ALL-SOUL, ALL-BODY, ALL-LOVE, ALL-POWER: A TRANSMYTHOLOGY

ALL-SOUL, ALL-BODY, ALL-LOVE, ALL-POWER: A TRANSMYTHOLOGY

P. Sufenas Virius Lupus

The Red Lotus Library

March, 2012

The Red Lotus Library is the publication imprint of the Ekklesía Antínoou, a queer, Graeco-Roman-Egyptian syncretist reconstructionist polytheist group dedicated to Antinous, the deified lover of the Roman Emperor Hadrian, and related divine figures.

The Red Lotus Library
Anacortes, WA, U.S.A.

Copyright © 2012 by P. Sufenas Virius Lupus

Printed by CreateSpace in the United States of America

DEIS NOVIS QVADRIS
PANPSYCHEI PANHYLEI
PANEROTEI PANCRATEI
ET DEO HEROIQVE ANTINOO
HERO POLYDEUKIONI
SANCTO LUCIO MARIO VITALI
DEO SETI
ET ALIIS DEIS MVLTIS
ROMANORVM GRAECORVM AEGYPTORVM
ET ALIIS GENTIBVS
PRO POPVLIS ECCLESIAE ANTINOI
P. SVF. VIRI. LVP. HVNC LIBRVM
DED. L.
DIES NATALIS PANCRATEI
MDCCCLXXXI P.M.A.
V • S • L • M
HAEC EST VNDE VITA VENIT

To all of the trans women and men
that I've had the good fortune to meet,
and to all of the metagender,
pangender, and genderqueer people
that I've known;
and to all the trans, meta-, pan-,
genderqueer and gender-diverse people
in the world, who are reading this,
and who are not reading it;
and to the memory of all those
who have not lived to see this:

The Tetrad are your divine parents;
but just as equally,
_WE_ are the ones who have given them birth.

Table of Contents

Preface and Acknowledgements

The work which follows here was the result of slightly more than a year's toil, from initial inspiration through to final publication. I have relied upon the material support of my own parents, friends, and other family members to a very large extent throughout this period, since regular employment and all of its benefits has been elusive, despite my best efforts.

I have benefited in the meantime from the good counsel, ears, eyes, minds, and hearts of a number of people, who have given encouragement, heard or read drafts of this work, given divination, or have been in other ways friendly and well-disposed toward this work, for which I am most grateful. I would like to name them here: Michael Sebastian Lvx, Sannion, Stephanopotamos, Andrew Carlson, Sarah Thompson, Lady Yeshe Rabbit, Chris Lee Vermeers, Ash Charlton, Lee Harrington, and many people whose proper names I do not know that wrote in and commented on the Aedicula Antinoi blog entries I've written detailing the Tetrad.

I also thank Nicole Hernandez, Michael Sebastian Lvx, and Jory Mickelson for their artistic contributions to the present volume: Nicole for the front cover and two internal pictures, Michael for the back cover, and Jory for his beautiful picture of Antinous that accompanies the beginning of the story. May all of the gods bless and favor the work of these wonderful individuals!

Introduction: Gods, Magic, Myth, and Modernity

Like all stories of birth, this one starts before the birth itself, with the first inklings that something was to be born. This occurred at PantheaCon 2011, when on Sunday the 20th of February,[1] I had a lot casting in which I was told that I would be creating "something new" in the next year in regards to my spirituality, and somehow the god Set would be heavily involved in it. I had a sense that the Serpent Path[2] would be involved in this new creation somehow, and I was correct...but, that was not the half of it.

The entire issue of trans-inclusion at PantheaCon 2011 (and, subsequently, at PantheaCon 2012) and in modern paganism more widely had many and varying results after the convention in '11, particularly in the pagan blogosphere. Then, around March 1st of that year, a post appeared on a blog by Foxfetch, and I read

---

[1] When the first draft of this essay was written as a blog post, on November 20, 2011, it was exactly nine months to the date from which this entire process had its unseen beginnings to its initial release into the wider world. The post can be found at http://aediculaantinoi.wordpress.com/2011/11/20/gods-magic-myth-and-modernity .

[2] I hope to detail more on the Serpent Path in future publications, and on my blog, where some information is already available about it.

1

it with great interest.[3] **"I demand transcentric imagery**, gods and goddesses with the wide variety of trans bodies, trans genitals, trans selves....I want us to **take our gods back**....We have mysteries *you have not dreamed of*. And we are **taking our magic back**. We are finding gods in our own image..."

On the night of March 2nd, something strange happened to me, which I then reported in vague terms to some people on March 3rd. I had what I can only call an experience of "spiritual birth"—and by that, I don't mean that I was in some way "spiritually re-born," but instead that I *gave birth* to several spiritual entities. While a great deal of it occurred in an unexpected (and unsought) altered state of consciousness, there was also a physical component to it as well: I had the strangest pains in my abdominal region that I have ever had in my life before (and I've had some bad incidents of what medical practitioners call "occult abdominal pain"—their own terms!—that had me in the hospital previously), but not like any of those...This lasted for several hours, and at the end of it, I knew that there were three entities that then existed that had not existed previously, or at least were not known to exist previously. I set about trying to learn more about these entities. I made an allusion to the beginnings of this work in a blog post on March 14th.[4] Over the days that came, I was able to figure out the names of these three entities...

However, as early as March 9th, I posed the following question to Sannion's oracle of Dionysos, giving Sannion no elaborations nor indications of what was going on:

What are your thoughts on Panpsyche, Panhyle, and Paneros?

And on March 17th, the answer came:

You are on the right track with these but there is a fourth you have yet to discover. The

---

[3] That post has subsequently been published as an essay called "Awakening the Transsexual Gods" in the excellent anthology edited by Calyxa Omphalos, Jacobo Polanshek, Gina Pond, Philip Tanner, and Sarah Thompson, *Gender and Transgender in Modern Paganism* (Cupertino, CA: Circle of Cerridwen Press, 2012), pp. 41-43.

[4] http://aediculaantinoi.wordpress.com/2011/03/14/an-anthology-on-gender-issues-in-modern-paganism/

2

next time you sacrifice to Antinous pay attention and full understanding will come to you. There can be no completeness without the Fourth.

Time progressed, and I was able to discern that the fourth entity came from the previous three, and I was able to determine that it had four names: a name that each of its three parents had given it, and a name that it took for itself. I was working on a poetic telling of a myth which detailed the complicated conception and birth of all of these figures. I discussed it in detail with a good friend and co-religionist of mine, and I also discussed some of these developments in brief with an artist, dear friend, and co-religionist.

Other people I tried to tell about these developments, I have literally never heard from again, while others with whom I'm still in contact ignored or interrupted me...but far greater were the number to whom I said nothing. I made allusions in vague manners to many people, asked if certain friends might be interested in reading something when I was finished with writing it (to which all agreed), and continued to slave away. I read the entirety of what I had written that March to Michael Sebastian Lvx, on a night during which we were constantly interrupted and distracted, and yet it was worthwhile to have done so.

I strove to return to the work, to continue writing it, and to finish it. I had hoped that by Transgender Day of Remembrance on November 20th, 2011, I would have had it finished in a form that would be accessible to everyone...But, because of the repeated delays with my previous book[5] and the emergence of a variety of other things (including a "day-job," such as it was) in the meantime, it was still not complete...But, I am getting ahead of myself.

In July of 2011, I had an oracular session with a dear friend, who has interceded on my behalf previously with the Ekklesía Antínoou *Sancti*, and in particular with the *Trophimoi*,[6] and it was in relation to the latter group that I was particularly inquiring in July. I received various insights from them (and some of

---

[5] P. Sufenas Virius Lupus, *Devotio Antinoo: The Doctor's Notes, Volume One* (Anacortes, WA: The Red Lotus Library, 2011).
[6] The three foster-sons of Herodes Attikos: Achilles, Memnon, and Polydeukion, of whom the third was given a widespread hero cultus in the second through fourth centuries CE.

my other ancestors) as a result of that oracular session; but, completely unexpectedly, I also received the following message on July 21st. Keep in mind that this oracle knew nothing of my work on the matter of the group of deities I have come to refer to as the Tetrad.

A group of spirits – all very tall and willowy, long hair, indeterminate gender. They're dancing in a circle, and chanting something I can't make out. They have a message for you from someone in your Antinoan pantheon (they won't tell me who): take time for yourself; treat yourself as well as you treat the spirits. Disrespecting yourself disrespects them. The spirits are very happy with you, and want you to receive your own love and devotion just as they do. They know this is hard, but you must do this. Begin with small steps until you become accustomed.

I knew immediately who these particular individuals were—the four entities to whom I had (partially) given birth...and the further member of the Antinoan pantheon they were speaking of, I am quite certain, is also involved in their birth: Lucius Marius Vitalis, one of the *Treiskouroi*, who had been intimately (quite literally!) involved in this entire process as well.

On October 29th of 2011, when I was a part of a divination session that Michael Sebastian Lvx had the night before Foundation Day,[7] in which we spoke with Anubis, there was a "private matter" which I omitted on my report of that occasion in the blog. This private matter was my question, "Do you have any advice on Panpsyche, Panhyle, Paneros, and Pancrates?" The answer we received was: *A six-pointed star traveling toward the western horizon.* You will have seen a rendering of that star in the frontispiece of this book by me, and a far more beautiful one by Michael Sebastian Lvx on the back cover of this book.[8]

---

[7] Foundation Day, October 30th, is the most important holy day of the Ekklesía Antínoou each year, celebrating the founding of the cultus of Antinous just after his death by drowning in 130 CE, and the foundation of his holy city of Antinoöpolis in Egypt. For more on this divination session, see the blog entry at http://aediculaantinoi.wordpress.com/2011/10/30/divination/

[8] The biggest difference between them is that he used Coptic letters, whereas I used Greek. Either one can work, certainly; perhaps those who are more accustomed to working with runes, ogam, or another orthographic system—including, indeed, English—can adapt the layout of the sigil for their own purposes however they might wish to do so.

4

So, you might be wondering: what, exactly, am I relating here? In the simplest and most accurate terms, I'm telling you about four new deities that I've "discovered," who are deities that are directly related to issues of transsexuality, transgender, and gender-variance in general. And, their story in mythic form is the subject of this book.

The first of these is Panpsyche, and she is a male-to-female transsexual/transgender deity, with all of the characteristics expectable at any and every stage of this process. One aspect of her—which, note, I am not suggesting is something that is involved with every male-to-female trans individual, but is simply something that she often presents—is a desire to be identified more with her soul and her inner being than with what her bodily configuration happens to be at any given moment, hence her name "Panpsyche," *All-Soul*. One of her symbols is the eagle, and she is associated most strongly with the element of Air.

Panhyle is the second individual, and is the twin brother of Panpsyche, except he is a female-to-male transsexual/transgender deity, with all the characteristics expectable at any and every stage of that process. One aspect of him is that he is extremely "grounded," very physical, and very much attached to physicality as an important dimension of one's personhood, hence his (not perfectly Greek, but nonetheless...!?!) name "Panhyle," *All-Body*, coming from a Greek term that means something more like "all-matter." One of his symbols is the bull, and he is most strongly associated with the element of Earth.

Note that both Panpsyche and Panhyle were born as a woman and as a man respectively, even though their bodily forms have not always matched their identities. This has not been a problem for them, nor for most of the other deities that have encountered them (and especially for the deities who helped to give birth to them), but it has been a problem for some people, both in the divine realms and in this world among their many trans men and trans women children.

Panpsyche and Panhyle have not always gotten along particularly well, but once they settled their differences at one point, they retreated behind closed doors, and when they emerged, they had given birth to a further being, Paneros—though neither Panhyle nor Panpsyche will say who "fathered" the new deity, nor who "birthed" it; indeed, the reality is that these terms are rather obsolete in relation to how Paneros came about.

Paneros is metagendered (which some might consider non-gendered), and while e[9] has characteristics that could be applied to any gender, e is not interested in identifying with any conventional gender as currently known in most human cultures. However, Paneros is interested in every gender and every person, and can be said to be quite flirtatious and promiscuous, even though eir affections often confuse and confound many people more than they may delight them. Paneros' name means *All-Love*, and one of eir symbols is the snake; Paneros' primary element is Water.

The final being in this new Tetrad of deities is complex, and was the result of the efforts of all three of the others working together—each can be said to have "fathered" this final being, and each can be said to have "given birth" to hir,[10] and yet none of them fathered nor gave birth to this being either in any way that would be recognizable by humans and most deities currently operating. This final being was called Panaletheia, "All-Truth," by Panhyle; Panpsyche called hir Paneirene, "All-Peace"; Paneros called hir Pankalos, "All-Beauty"; but this being named hirself Pancrates, *All-Power*. Pancrates (not to be confused with the magician/poet/priest Pachrates of Heliopolis, who is also called Pancrates in Greek sources; in the present work, I always distinguish them by calling the Egyptian magician Pachrates) can be described as pangendered (or, in the views of some people, as androgynous), and exhibits characteristics that could be found in every and any gender, both mentally, behaviorally, spiritually, and physically. One of Pancrates' symbols is the lion, and hir elemental association is Fire.

While—like every good deity worthy of the name—the parentage of these four deities is multiple, and could exist in a variety of versions (on which, more in a moment), a great many deities were involved in the conceptions and birth of them. Antinous, Polydeukion of the *Trophimoi*, and Favorinus of Arles were all very important in this process, and Pan (whose name is contained in the names

---

[9] I use Old Spivak pronouns for Paneros. These, briefly, are e (subject), em (object), eir (possessive), emself (reflexive).

[10] For Pancrates, I use the "transgendered" pronouns sie (subject) and hir (object, possessive).

of all four of the Tetrad) himself had a very essential role to play; likewise, on the side of goddesses, Artemis had a very interesting and essential role to play.[11] However, the original twins were carried to term (though it was a rather strange and short term, granted—these are gods, after all!) by Set, and the last being besides Set to have a direct "hand" (or perhaps another bodily member!) in their physical creation was Lucius Marius Vitalis.

Π • Π • Π • Π

And so you think that the sun is jealous of the evening-star, or that it matters to him what star beside is in the sky? Not thus is it with this mighty fire. For it seems to me that, like the poet, he assigns his portion to each, saying: To thee I give the North and to thee the South, to thee the evening, but in the darkness of night are ye all, yea all, when I am invisible.... [12]

—Philagrus, in Philostratus' *Lives of the Sophists*

One of the things that I like the best about polytheism is that **there are a lot of deities**...and by this, I don't mean something as trifling as the "Twelve Olympians," nor the 200,000 deities sometimes said to be reckoned amongst the Hindus, nor even the eight million *kami* spoken of in Shinto. Why would there be a limited number of deities, no matter how large those limits happen to be? And while I wouldn't likewise suggest that there are an infinite number of deities, I wouldn't be surprised if there is somewhere closer to that number than to even tens or hundreds of millions of them, particularly if we count land spirits, abstract concepts, heroes, ancestors, totem animals, and other such beings into the mix...

The reality is, there are deities who were once worshipped on the earth who we

---

[11] Some might read into this aspect of the story the historical facts of PantheaCon 2011 and 2012, involving some trans discriminatory acts and transphobic language on the part of certain Dianic groups and individuals. While I would not say that this is the primary motivation for Artemis' appearance in the narrative, one can certainly read it as a theological and ethical statement in light of those events.

[12] Wilmer Cave Wright (ed./trans.), *Philostratus, Lives of Sophists; Eunapius, Lives of Philosophers* (Cambridge, MA: Harvard University Press, 1921), p. 213.

have forgotten entirely, and may never be able to recall or recover, and yet I would maintain that they still exist. Likewise, why should we assume that we have exhausted the total store of deities that there are in all of our human knowledge of mythology and religion worldwide? And, as I am someone involved in both process theology and polyamorotheism,[13] I don't think there's any barrier to new deities that have never been encountered previously coming into being. Indeed, every deity currently known and widely reckoned had to have had an "entry" into their culture of origin at some point. Why would this process have stopped in the modern period, when it has never stopped previously? Especially now, when there are concepts and ideas and forces with which we deal on a regular basis that have never been encountered previously, why would older and previously known deities simply be re-assigned to them? As much as Hermes and Athena may have some connection to the internet, and may even claim some patronage over it or even to have invented it themselves, I suspect the Internet has a very different deity behind it, that actually runs it on a day-to-day basis. It may look like a very big and well-connected bionic spider at the center of its worldwide web, slowly luring each of us in, to stray down paths we never thought we would, getting more and more tangled, and even luring some to their doom...Or, it may be a factory floor of a million monkeys tapping away endlessly at a million typewriters, each monkey as equally divine as all the others, and each as insane, and each typewriter likewise...but I digress!

Many deities have been asserted as "trans-deities" in the past. These have included, amongst others, Attis, Shiva, Loki, Hermaphroditos, and a variety of other possibilities. But, the reality of trans-ness in the modern world is something quite different from all of the myths and cultural realities of most of these deities. This is not to say that these deities are not gender-variant: they are. Nor is it to say that trans people may not be interested in these deities, and identify with them to a degree, nor that the deities themselves may take an interest in trans people: they certainly do and most definitely have. Foxfetch makes the distinction in his writing that trans deities are not the same as third-gender or androgynous deities, and this is very important to keep in mind. Far too often, I've heard trans people referred to as "androgynous" or as in some way perfectly combining male and female "polarities," when in reality they are men or women,

---

[13]   http://www.patheos.com/Resources/Additional-Resources/Polytheology-Syncretism-Process-Theology-and-Polyamorotheism.html

but their bodies don't match the common understandings and recognitions of those genders. Thus, it is important to keep in mind that the modern understanding of trans-ness is something that is quite new. If "homosexuality" as defined in the modern world is only about 150 years old, trans-ness (including the medical processes that can assist it) is less than a century.

The appropriation of many gender-variant deities or spiritual roles by queer (but often specifically gay) men has been common for the last several decades, and yet inclusion of trans people in queer struggles or social consciousness even within spiritual contexts has not always accompanied such appropriations. Further, some people have even taken it upon themselves to "assign" what deities are appropriate for trans people to recognize and identify with, in manners that are entirely inappropriate, inadequate, or even offensive to trans people's own senses of identity. As Foxfetch demanded that there be trans deities, so I think it is very much time that many such deities—both the ones I've outlined here and many others besides—come forward into being and knowledge for people.

But, Foxfetch mentioned that some might find the idea of the deities they already know adopting trans forms to be blasphemous, and then said "*fuck that noise*." While I do think this approach is the correct one, I am also aware that it would be just as foreign for us to force some deity that has been long-held to have a male or a female form and identity suddenly have a different identity, as it is for wider society, our parents, religious leaders, and others to force trans people to be, dress as, and act like the genders they're "supposed to be." Let us not make a procrustean bed of trans issues and force deities of the past onto it, let us instead awaken trans and other gender-variant deities from their own beds! There is no possibility for blasphemy against existing powers and their human followers if the deities in question are our own, and if we never have to "take them back," because they have always been ours to begin with.

I would assert that, even when some deities may have pre-existed the work of poets and other artists who have treated them in their writings, paintings, sculptures, songs, dances, dramas, and other arts, it is the portrayals of deities through art that has been the force that has often fixed them in human culture and consciousness, that has lured in potential devotees and worshippers, and that has often endeared them to humans long before the humans concerned have had a personal encounter with the deity-in-question. While there are prophets who have announced their deities in various ways, the ones who have done so with art and with compelling narrative and creative expression have done so in ways far superior to those who have sought to enforce their new (and often "reforming") prophecies with force, intimidation, domination, and subjugation. I would go as far as to suggest that it is the words of poets, of artists, and of such creative craftspersons that is the primary medium via which the gods have come to be known in the world amongst humans. In this manner, as Philagrus says above in Philostratus' work, poets are not like the sun, but instead the sun is like a poet, illuminating each of the stars in their orbit...

However, I wish to emphasize that I am no prophet, and I refuse to be in any way even considered in the same category as "prophets." I have been in the odd position of having had experiences of these particular deities, four "new" deities that have perhaps existed previously but have not been given name or form or characteristics until quite recently, and yet they are independent of me, and their existences have been confirmed by oracular readings independent of myself, in two of three cases of which the human oracles in question had no knowledge whatsoever about the nature of the beings or the work in which I was involved when the questions were asked. Indeed, ancient divine heroes and new deities throughout the Greek and Roman world often had less "confirmation" of their divine status in many cases that prompted communities to give them cultus. These deities are here, they exist, and they are accessible to anyone who wishes to reach out to them and learn more about them. I'm still involved in the process of learning more about them myself.

Some might suggest that what I am doing here is hubris, or that such "innovations" are to be shunned. Yes, I am a reconstructionist, but I am well aware that I do not live in ancient Greece, Rome, Egypt, Britain, Ireland, or any other location, no matter how appealing all of those might be (at least in theory). The world has changed, the gods have changed along with it, and as a process theologian, I have no reason to doubt that more gods have come about as a result of those changes. I think it is far more hubristic, personally, to assume that human knowledge—no matter how great, wondrous, and beautiful the boundaries, depths, and heights of it happen to be—has determined the extent of the gods already, and that nothing more that may be useful or productive or appealing may come about in terms of adding to the roll-call of the gods

10

currently known. But, this is another of the great advantages of the polytheistic religious viewpoint: one need not honor *all the gods*, but only the ones that are relevant to oneself, or that have reached out to one.

Some might also object to how promiscuously syncretistic and cross-cultural the following myth is. For any future TransMythology, I think such syncretism is going to be the norm rather than the exception. The prefix "trans-" does not just apply to gender issues in everyday life; its basic meaning is "across." Therefore, for a TransMythology to likewise cross the (supposed) barriers between cultures—barriers which have been more conceptual and artificial rather than on-the-ground realities, both in the ancient world and now—seems to me both natural and expectable.

As polytheists, we certainly have theology (despite the objection of some in the modern pagan community to that term's supposed "Christian" connotations) and philosophy, both in the modern period and historically. But, perhaps even more—and more preferable—than these, we have mythology, which is redolent with theology and philosophy, whether we wish it to be or not. As much as the essays in *Gender and Transgender in Modern Paganism* are important and, indeed, essential parts of this discussion, as well as all of the blog entires across the pagan blogosphere, very few of these "sing" in the way that myths should. If Foxfetch demands that we have trans deities, then the deities need to have a story. What follows is one such story.

I know that, no matter how beautiful or stirring or moving the mythic poetic narrative I produce about Panhyle, Panpsyche, Paneros and Pancrates happens to be, I cannot bring about the further "birthing" of these gods alone: it takes a community to do so, not only of potential devotees, but of artists of all types. I would love for there to be no "canonical" version of their myths or their depictions; I would love to see diversity, plurality, and great and wondrous variety in how people speak of them, show them, sing of them, and so forth. While my work on them may be the "earliest" chronologically, I do not want what I write on them to be the "last word," by any means.

I have no illusions whatsoever that this is not the end of the story for the Tetrad—their stories are only beginning with this offering of first-fruits. Further,

I have no illusions that this is, or will be, the *ur*-text version of the Tetrad's story. It will only be possible to maintain that kind of pretense until such a time as another writer, poet, or artists puts pen to paper, finger to keyboard, brush to canvas, palm to clay, hand to instrument, or breath to song to further their story, or provide alternate versions. This version of their story will be no more "definitive" in terms of their overall mythology as the *Homeric Hymns* are in comparison to Hesiod, or as Callimachus is in comparison to pseudo-Apollodorus, or as Vergil to Diodorus Siculus—in other words, it will only be academics concerned with doctoral dissertations, disciplinary boundaries, and the limits of their syllabi that will attempt to state what is and is not "canonical" when it comes to the Tetrad.

I fully expect that a trans woman, for example, will relate the story of Panpsyche differently than I have; a trans man will tell Panhyle's tale in his own way; and a pangendered person will narrate the adventures of Pancrates in ways I cannot fathom. Indeed, I even expect that other metagender people will speak of Paneros' trials and triumphs along much more unexpected lines than I have. Each will also speak of the other deities in the Tetrad in ways particular to themselves. And, we can only wonder how a genderqueer person might choose to relate any of these stories—or, for that matter, a cisgendered person of any gender! I look forward to the time when they will, and welcome all who wish to labor towards those ends.

All of those future myths are equally true and valid, as long as they carry true devotion to these deities and convey the viewpoint of the person who tells the myth as truly and honestly and as authentically as possible. This means that no myth can invalidate any other version of the myth, even though the details might contradict or be at variance with other versions. Polytheistic societies have always been polyvalent in their narrative strategies, and "both/and" is always a more viable reality than "either/or" where such things are concerned.

Nine months exactly after the first indications of their coming into being, and more than eight months after the night in early March in which I suffered through abdominal pains and headaches,[14] I mentioned the existence of the

---

[14] Which, I would note, repeated on November 20th, 2011 when I first announced the Tetrad to a wider public; and, in the final days of preparing the present manuscript,

Tetrad to the wider world. A year on from their initial birth, between the birth-festivals of Panpsyche, Panhyle, and Paneros on March 2nd and the birth-festival of Pancrates on March 17th, I feel it is now time to release them into the world as widely as possible in mythic form, to have whatever effect they might have on whomever else might come to hear of them, take an interest in them, and come to love them as much as I have loved them. Though I cannot send them forth equipped with the fully-fledged spiritual complex of myth, song, dance, and iconography that I had hoped they would have, I can offer what I have offered here in the present volume.

In the meantime, write poems about them, write songs about them, write stories about them, draw and paint pictures of them, dance for them, build shrines for them, call them forth into your sacred spaces, and do whatever you might wish with them...

Π • Π • Π • Π

Based on Anubis' advice, the sigil or symbol for them is a six-pointed star. The Greek letter *pi* is in the middle, standing for their four names. In the top triangle is a *sigma* for Set, and in the bottom is a *lambda* for Lucius Marius Vitalis. In the other four triangles are the letters *upsilon* for the -*hyle* in Panhyle (note that in Greek, "h" is not a letter but instead a rough-breath mark in words beginning with vowels), a *psi* for the -*psyche* in Panpsyche, an *epsilon* for the -*eros* in Paneros, and a *kappa* for the -*crates* in Pancrates. It may not be as elegant or as beautiful as it could possibly be...but, if you feel that it should be better, and you can in some manner *make it better*, then feel free to take up this torch and do so however you see fit. Indeed, Michael Sebastian Lvx's version on the back cover of this book is quite beautiful.

Π • Π • Π • Π

---

between the Tetrad's birth-dates of March 2 (for Panpsyche, Panhyle, and Paneros) and March 17 (for Pancrates), I had a sore throat and a neuropathy flare-up. The voice of Panpsyche, and the feet of Panhyle, get featured rather heavily in the myth to follow, particularly at their birth!

Praise to all of the gods, heroes, ancestors, and Sancti on this day—but especially to Antinous, Polydeukion, Set, and Lucius Marius Vitalis for giving birth to the new gods, the Tetrad: Hail Panpsyche! Hail Panhyle! Hail Paneros! Hail Pancrates!

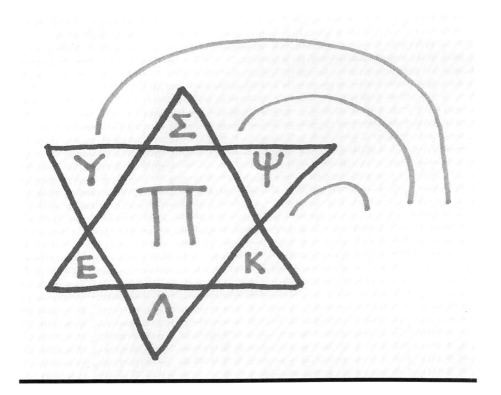

All-Soul, All-Body, All-Love, All-Power

I.

Antinous reclined against Hadrian's chest,
while Achilles and Memnon wrestled;
Lucius Marius Vitalis intently listened
to Julia Balbilla's latest recitation for Sabina;
Herodes Attikos and Favorinus of Arles debated,
while Polydeukion interjected on philosophy
between Matidia and Plotina, Marciana and Domitia Paulina,
as Trajan feigned interest in their discussion,
instead turning his eyes to the youths.

"It occurs to me, love," Antinous mused aloud,
"that of all present, only two have had children."

Each of the gathered deified mortals and heroes
stopped at this, turning their attention to the Bithynian.

Appia Annia Regilla and her daughters,
Elpinike and Athenais, and young Regillus,
joined the group at this moment of silence.

"Tell me truly, Herodes, in the spirit of inquiry,
do you think it was a blessing to have had children?"

"My young friend, your frankness disarms me,
and in good conscience I cannot but reply with frankness.
The joy that my children brought me cannot be measured,
nor can the grief that I endured at their deaths be plumbed,
nor can the disappointment that he who outlived me
be ranked and reckoned, much to my own dismay...
Which proves, by the gods, that the mystery of parenthood
is that none can know, when undergoing it,
what the results may be—happiness, sadness, or regret;
and yet, making the attempt was never a cause for remorse.
If our fates were known at every turn,
what use would life's moments unfolding in turn be?"

"That's easy for you to say, husband," Regilla began,
"for what came through me from the gods
cannot in any manner be compared
to the experience of what came through you.
Even a mediocre baker can toss together dough,
but without perfection of time baking in a good oven,
the best baker's dough can be blackened and burnt.
Nine months of waiting, of carrying,
nine hours of pain and of utmost labor,
this, which you have not experienced and cannot comprehend,
it is *this* which makes a mother love each child."

"And yet," Sabina interjected, "not every mother loves,
nor does every father remain removed from his children."

Matidia spoke hastily, "But I love both of my daughters!"
Marciana spoke after, "And I my daughter and grand-daughters!"
Athenais added, "And father loved us well, certainly!"

18

Laughing, Sabina continued, "I neither indict nor critique
any among this good company for lacking in love
nor in due attention given to children born.
Lacking children myself, however, I must comment
that love can be known in other ways,
and that children chosen, rather than birthed,
can be as dear as those from one's own flesh."
"You were called '*Diva*' in death, dear lady,"
Polydeukion responded, "but in life you were equally divine,
possessed of Athena's greatest gifts,
as well as of Eros' favor and Zeus' friendship."

"Boy, boy, boy," Trajan interrupted, "You are mistaken!
Though Eros favors all, Zeus' virtues are manly,
thus never given to the fairer sex."

"'Fairer' in what sense, o divine emperor?"
All eyes turned to Favorinus, the eunuch orator.

"I would expect ignorance on your part, eunuch,
for what do you know of feminine fairness
nor of manly virtue? Nothing and neither!"

"If you wish to dispute, *Parthicus*,
lay on—but, pray that your tongue is as honeyed
as your spear-head was known for being bloodied."

"You, a pathetic *gallus*, would defy *me?*"

"I have defied other emperors and yet lived to speak of it—
as I am now beyond fear of death, I have nothing to lose...
But, be that as it may, I do defy you, and this I choose
because, it seems to me, you are in error in your words."

"By Jupiter, I shall have you dragged like Hector!"

"Hector all you like, *Imperator*—
words are powerful, more powerful than swords,
more sturdy than burnished brazen shields...
as I speak Greek, my words are winged
like the feet of Hermes, swift between ears of gods;
but as I am Gaulish, my words also carry a club
that, like Herakles, can slay lions or tame Cerberus."

Plotina stood between her fuming spouse
and the Gaulish orator as some gasped,
some were silent in shock, while the boys laughed.

Hadrian responded, "Surely, we are reasonable souls—
why must there be enmity between us?"

Domitia Paulina agreed with her brother, "Indeed, Hadrian—
though we often disagreed, our filial affection never waned."

"Then let us return," Antinous continued, "to my premise.
There is division between man and woman,
there is motherhood and there is fatherhood,
there is manliness and its perception,
there is womanliness and its exceptions...
there are mysteries in each of these positions,
and there is our friend, Favorinus,
who some say is not manly enough to be called a man,
but who is likewise not a woman—"

"Yet, I maintain," the Gaulish orator interrupted,
"that in speech and performance of my arts,
those unaware of what is beneath my clothes
would know no different if I played male or female."

"Which, if you would have let me finish, dear friend,
I would have allowed for as well!
There are more than simply two positions on this.
Like every mystery, these cannot be understood fully
outside of experiencing them as they unfold...

"Yet, who can point to one moment
when one's gender was experienced definitively?
That preparation for its mystery occurred
and then revelation, with all its glory, arrived?
Perhaps gender, then, is not so much a mystery to undergo
as much as a lens through which one sees the world."

There were sighs and sounds of approval,
though Achilles mostly wanted to wrestle again.
"Dear friends, we are beyond the boundaries of mortality now;
we are divine beings, immeasurable in power.
Nothing is out of our potential grasp.
Therefore, let us not squander this opportunity."

"What is it that you propose?" asked Hadrian.

"Is it not obvious?"

Confused and expectant gazes fell upon Antinous,
except for Polydeukion, who smiled in self-congratulation
at the scenario playing out in his head,
and Favorinus, who rolled his eyes and sighed,
amused, but also upset that he didn't think of it first.

"What is it to be a man or a woman?
Is it inherent in the body, as some think,
or is it a quality of soul, as others may know?"

Herodes interjected, "More questions?
We were expecting answers, dear boy!"

"The answer is forthcoming, Herodes!
Patience, a Stoic virtue, is not favored by you,
and yet, now it should be exercised!
What is it to have a child?
Is it a joy and a sorrow and a potential disappointment,
the experience of many a parent,
or is it an achievement of love after strife?"

Hadrian queried, "More questions?
There is also virtue in brevity, lover!"

"I'll remember that the next time
you wish to spend hours in love's embrace!
What is it to be divine?
The gods we have known and worshipped
have done the impossible, the improbable
at every turn, and yet the cosmos spins...
What divine potentials have we not yet tapped,
what feats may be achieved simply and only
because we have not allowed our imaginations—
the gift we had most in abundance from the gods—
to be as free nor as bold as we could have done?"

Memnon pleaded, "More questions?"
Matidia and Marciana cajoled, "More questions?"
Lucius Marius Vitalis whined, "More questions?"
Julia Balbilla and Domitia Paulina complained, "More questions?"
All challenged, "MORE QUESTIONS?!?"

But Polydeukion smirked, Favorinus rolled his eyes...
and Achilles kicked the dirt, because he wanted to wrestle.

"Dear friends, dear lovers, dear devoted divine beings—
we were human when we were upon the earth,
with its splendors and its trials,
with our limitations as well as our ecstasies;
but now, we are no longer upon the earth,
we are not like unto gods...
we are gods.
Let us act like it, therefore.
If there is an inherence in gender,
a mystery to be undergone
or a window through which to interpret,
then let the gods undergo it and see for themselves."

Trajan inquired, "Do you suggest, then,
that we...change our genders?"

Antinous laughed. "No, of course not!
Don't be silly! What good would that do?"

Hadrian pursued further, "Then what, love?"

"Speak along with me, Favorinus and Polydeukion:

"If the gods would know where gender resides
and whether it is window or revelation..."

"...then the gods must be the window,
must undergo the revelation..."

"...and though all the gods now in existence
may make this choice as they see fit for themselves..."

"...new gods may come forth, now,
to make these propositions into reality..."

"...and, whether or not we have previously known
birth and begetting, parenting or adoption..."

"...by our godly power, all of us together, and others,
may be the fathers and mothers of these new gods."

Everyone present stared in astonishment
at Antinous, Polydeukion, and Favorinus.

Stares became smiles, smiles became laughter,
glimmering eyes slitted to joyous squinting.

Horizons of mind were expanded,
potentials of bodies were exploded,
as if Dionysos sprang from thigh,
Athena burst from skull,
Kairos streamed from urethra,
Orion broke from skin-bag,
and Metis spoke from stomach
of the great god Zeus all at once.

But they would need assistance.

II.

It seemed that before their last syllable was a memory
another had joined their company.

It was an angel, luminous with silver wings
and scale-like feathers arrayed as thousands of daggers.

"A message for you:
a special council has been convened on this issue,
to which you are requested in immediate attendance."

The angel departed as swiftly as it had appeared.

The company, somewhat taken aback,
composed itself and prepared to travel thither thence.

Antinous and an ennead,
Polydeukion and an ogdoad:
Antinous, Hadrian, and Sabina,
Trajan, Plotina, and Julia Balbilla,
Marciana and Matidia, Favorinus and Domitia Paulina;
Polydeukion, Memnon, and Achilles,
Herodes Attikos and Appia Annia Regilla,
Elpinike, Athenais, and Regillus,
and Lucius Marius Vitalis.

The god Antinous was seated in the council's chambers first,
with the hero Polydeukion at right,
and the heroine Regilla to Polydeukion's right in turn;
Hadrian and his *Divae* next,
then Trajan and his *Divae*;
Vitalis with the two other *Trophimoi*;
Herodes and his two daughters;
and his son with the orator and the poetess.

There were at least thirty gods or more
Assembled in the chambers awaiting their arrival.

Osiris the Just and his wife Isis presided;
Hermes Trismegistos was the secretary.

Ibis-headed Thoth read out a statement.

"The company of favored mortals here assembled—
under the protection of the God Antinous,
the heroes Vibullius Polydeukion and Appia Annia Regilla,
Divus Hadrianus and *Divus* Traianus Parthicus,
Diva Sabina, *Diva* Plotina,
Diva Marciana, *Diva* Matidia
and *Diva* Domitia Paulina—
have been summoned before the present tribunal
to answer charges of hubris and treachery."

Assembled gods and the company of divine mortals
gasped in disbelief, confusion, and surprise.

"On what grounds are these charges leveled?"
Herodes Attikos questioned the tribunal.

"Silence!" cried Minos.
"You have no standing to speak before this assembly!"

Polydeukion rose gravely.
"I apologize to this august council
for the actions of my foster-father,
who meant no offense to your dignity.
Is it within our rights, perhaps,
to request legal counsel?"

"It is," Minos nearly spat.

A glance between Antinous and Polydeukion spoke volumes.

"We therefore," Polydeukion continued,
"wish to appoint as counsel for our defense
the god of good speech, friend to mortals,
patron of Arcadia, Hermes."

"I object!" screamed Minos!

"You have no grounds to object, Minos,"
Isis spoke slowly and without malice.

"I gratefully accept this appointment,
and will faithfully execute my duties
in the interests of the three ladies—
Justice, Peace, and Piety."

"Thank all the gods!"
Trajan whispered to Hadrian.

"YOU'RE WELCOME!"
all the gods present replied.

In what seemed like a wink,
Trajan clearly heard Hermes say
"Now is not the time to forget
that you are no longer mortal,
nor that where you are now
prayers travel even faster
than I am able to move and speak!"

"As the esteemed sophist and philanthropist requested,
the accused have the right to know in particular
the grounds for the charges against them."

"So noted," Osiris responded.
"Minos, proceed."

"The charge of hubris was incurred
when general assent amongst this group of mortals
agreed to conspire as divine abetters
to the plan of the god and the hero also here charged.

"The charge of treachery against divine order
was incurred when the group decided
to raise a new race of gods
without leave of the gods of Greece,
Rome, Egypt, or the wider cosmos."

"How do you answer these charges?"
Osiris' question hung like a storm cloud.

Herodes and Favorinus muttered quietly to one another,
Hadrian and Trajan exchanged angry and frustrated glances,
while Polydeukion and Antinous simply stared, dumbfounded.

"On the charge of hubris: not guilty.
On the charge of treachery: not guilty."

The assembled deified mortals gazed in amazement at Hermes' words.
In a quick glance toward them,
they all heard Hermes say,
"If your mind can think it,
I know it before your tongue can say it,
but only if you *want* to say it...
Communication takes place between two things,
and even within your singular selves
are thousands of individual faculties
speaking and receiving messages constantly...

"I am there for every single one.
In the interests of time, therefore,
and because I know the gods' laws,
I will speak as necessary
without conferring with you—
you need only confer inside yourselves.
Aren't you glad you picked me?
Athena, for her legal savvy, would have been great,
but she can't do *this*!"

"Do you deny," Isis asked,
"the actions which lead to these charges."

"Not at all, honorable judges;
merely their interpretation."

"What nonsense is this?" Minos countered.

"I intend to demonstrate definitively,
with neither deception nor trickery,
that while the facts in this matter
may indeed be as the prosecution establishes,
that we are in no way obligated
to therefore consider those facts,
those actions willfully undertaken,
to constitute either treachery or hubris."

"Very well, then," Osiris answered.
"The prosecution may proceed."

Minos stood before Osiris and Isis.

"Honored judges, respected gods—
I am compelled to pursue the charge
of hubris first and foremost.
This god—the one god amongst this company—
incited his companions into thinking
the power of the gods was their own.

"This is grotesque, unbelievable, bizarre, and unprecedented,
excessive in every possible fashion,
and the very essence of hubris."

"How does the defense wish to respond?"
Isis spoke, with Osiris scrutinizing
the assembled deified mortals and justified dead closely.

"With three questions, honored judges."
Hermes' eyes glimmered, smiling at Antinous.
"First, is Antinous rightly called
'Antinous-Osiris the Justified'?"

"Objection!" Minos exclaimed.

"Overruled!" Osiris replied sternly.
"The question is appropriate,
and the answer affirmative."

"Second, then," Hermes continued,
"to be 'justified' implies a soundness
of judgment, of action, and of intention
in the sight of the gods
and in accordance with Ma'at,
does it not?"

"Again, the answer is affirmative,"
Isis responded.

"Then finally, third," Hermes proceeded,
"if Antinous-Osiris the Justified
spoke in a manner that suggested
his companions are possessed of divine power,
is it even possible that his perception
could have been in the least incorrect?"

Silence fell over the council's chambers.

"Therefore," Hermes concluded,
"the divine joy felt by the prospect of future action
which this group of deified mortals experienced
was neither false, nor ill-suited to their states,
or else it would not have been able to occur.
Thus, to be blunt, hubris is not possible in this situation."

"Honored judges, I object! I object! I object!"

"No, I OBJECT!"

Everyone turned in surprise
to see Lucius Marius Vitalis standing.

"If what Hermes says is true,
then I and my companions
who are not gods, heroes, nor divine emperors
have as much standing in this tribunal
as any god, hero, or divine emperor.
If Minos can be a prosecutor,
and our actions are fit to be judged by gods,
then our divinity must be equal to theirs,
even if it is not as long-standing."

"Insolence!" Minos spat.

"No—truth."
Isis spoke, and Minos sat down.
"The charge of hubris, therefore,
cannot stand.
Proceed with the second count."

Hermes smiled at his charges,
and each heard him say,
"Nicely done, kid, but you
didn't have to go there—
you've earned their respect,
but you could have been destroyed.

"This second charge
is going to be a breeze
compared with that one,
so just sit tight!"

"Honored judges, revered powers,
the charge of treachery—
while its results can be easily met
by your able and superlative might—
is perhaps even more serious.
These conspirators, in their folly,
have expressed a wish
to raise a new race of gods
to which they would give birth...
Gods who might challenge your supremacy,
gods who might vie for your positions,
gods who might usurp your powers,
gods who might steal devotions from you!
By all the gods, I charge them thus,
and suggest they be punished
for even *thinking* to attempt something like this!"

"The first objection I raise, honored judges,
is one of semantics in my opponent's charge:
he has both appealed to your *might*,
but also his scenario relies upon *might*—
not *will*, not *have*, not anything substantial.
Unless my opponent is possessed of oracular insight
(which he is concealing!)
and knows this scenario of suspicion is true—
whereupon he is lying and therefore culpable—
his creation of an atmosphere of fear
is entirely unwarranted in this context."

"Are you calling me a liar?" Minos retorted.

"No; simply a poor diviner.

"Among the gods there are better diviners than you,
therefore I call upon my brother, Pythios Apollon,
to prognosticate accurately where you have feebly conjectured."

Golden Apollon, like a shower of honey,
came forward from the throng of gods.
"Brother, is there any truth at all
to the suspicions Minos has raised?"

"No."

"Thank you. Nothing further."

As a light breeze across laurel leaves
Apollon returned to the crowd of deities.

"Yet my concerns are valid!
Is it not the utmost treachery
to suggest that the many gods,
both present and elsewhere in the universe,
are not sufficient for what is in the universe?"

"Have the gods grown so insecure, Minos,
in not-even-two millennia of neglect
to be as petty as to fight over devotees,
and to see the very existence of variety
not as beautiful diversity, but instead as competition?"

"If I concede your point, Hermes,
I still maintain that the multitude
of gods that now exist
can successfully oversee all that may come about."

"Even if that were true,
change is inevitable, and thus adaptation as well.
If you wish to give up your duties
as judge of the dead to instead
patronize purveyors of Nigerian SPAM scams,
please do so with my blessings.

"Many gods may not wish to change their interests,
so new gods for new concerns are welcome.
That should answer your reservations at last."

"NO! This matter is not yet settled!
What monstrosities might arise from these mortals?"
Minos' continued pursuit of the issue was pathetic.

"Nothing greater than what monstrosities
have also come forth from the gods—
is not Typhon the child of Hera alone?"

"But how can an immortal god
come forth from lowly mortals?"

"Is not Dionysos as we know him now
immortal from a formerly-mortal mother?"

"Mortal—even in lineage of an immortal—
cannot beget an immortal!"

"And yet, here stands Antinous,
late of Bithynia, distant descendant
of my own blood through Pan of Arcadia
in his ancestry of Antinoë of Mantineia.
If you dispute his divinity,
you would run afoul of Osiris himself."

"But, begetting after death
brings sorrow and ruin!"

"If you refer to Euphorion,
child of Helen and Achilleus
in their abode of the Blessed Isle,
struck down by your father's thunderbolt..."

"I do! Treachery, and the just
punishment of a clear threat!"

"No—jealousy, the spiteful smiting
of what could not be possessed...
and you will find, Minos,
that the death-within-death
which Euphorion underwent
was not to his detriment,
for he is even still among us,
just as Asklepios, thunder-struck, is.
Nothing and no one is ever lost."

"But...it isn't right!"

"If it were not right, Minos,
then you would likewise have no standing here,
though Zeus himself is your father.
Do not continue in resentment
at these, who eluded your judgment in death—
they are all justified under Antinous the God."

Osiris struck his sceptre
against the ground four times.
"My esteemed wife, the foundation of my justice,
and I have conferred on this matter.
The charge of treachery is dismissed
on lack of evidence."

The deified mortals all rose and cried out,
exclaiming in celebration of their favorable verdict.

"But wait!"

They fell silent and turned again to Osiris.

"Giving birth to new gods is a difficult matter.
You have not experienced it previously.
Though your intentions are pure,
and your powers are formidable,
even your assembled group
cannot do this alone.

"You will need help.

"We, therefore, attach this condition
to the exoneration of your group from all accusations:
whoever among gods, heroes, and deified mortals
that may wish to join in your endeavor,
including all of those present here,
is obliged to do so forthwith,
including ourselves."

Polydeukion spoke again.
"Honored judges, we would wish nothing other,
and are pleased and thankful for your assistance."

III.

They did not depart from the chambers,
but continued their presence there
under different auspices and purposes;
the thrones of judgment were now simply seats,
the juridical gallery of gods now a peaceful parliament.

Into the assembly came a shorn-headed Egyptian
in linen vestments with a leopard-skin sash.
Antinous and Hadrian recognized him immediately.

"The Divine Ones wish to create a new god—
this is an activity that I am familiar with,
and therefore I shall lend my assistance."

"We are at your mercy, Pachrates," Antinous said,
"direct us as you see fit."

"Very well...

"Friends, to give life to a new god
is no small nor mean feat to attempt;
though many of the gods have done so before
with little or no thought to the consequences
nor future implications of their acts,
today will be different entirely.
Never has a company of more beings come together
for the creation of one being.

"Pandora received all the gifts of the gods,
the first female of the human race—
but this new being will also be
a gift to all, as she was,
under the parentage and patronage of many,
and unlike her, begotten rather than built.

"The matter of gestating and birthing
is, at present, a side concern;
what is necessary in the meantime
is a container strong enough to hold
every drop and spark of divine power,
perhaps adding its own elements to the mix in the process.
I can think of no better candidate
for this difficult but important role
than the god who is already *all*: Pan."

Goat-eared Pan came forth, shaggy,
and stood before everyone.

"It is my pleasure to be everyone's pleasure."

"Those who were formerly of the mortal race,
what follows will be difficult for you to understand.
Generation and begetting amongst the gods
does not happen as you may be accustomed to—
Pan will be acting as a vessel,
but a very unusual one.

"When the males take him from behind
and leave their divine seed with him
it will seem as though they have been ravished;
and when the females mount him
he will not leave anything within them,
but instead his phallus will draw out their divine essence
to add to the rest, and they shall feel spent
as if they were lustful sated satyrs.

"Even for the immortal gods, however,
a foundation in form is first necessary,
therefore the formerly mortal divinities
will give of themselves to Pan first.
Proceed as you like."

Every last one of the deified mortals
felt as though this was more of a lurid spectacle
than a divine undertaking;
but to the shameless gods
for whom concealment and revelation are as one
this entire situation, though unique,
was as pedestrian in its implications
as the merest thought for the cosmos' continuation.

Antinous, the instigator of these actions
and the only full-fledged god among the mortals,
knew that he must lead by example.
Leaving aside care and clothing,
he approached the waiting, grinning goat-god,
knocked him onto his back, spread his legs,
and with an erection like the finest polished crystal
he gently and lovingly fucked Pan, saying
"May this new god share in my beauty!"

There was not a being present
who found this sight upsetting,
and indeed many lingered in watching it
for the sheer ecstasy of seeing
such a beautiful scene unfolding before them.

Lucius Marius Vitalis, however,
did not merely want to watch.
With an enterprising spirit, the prince of the *Sancti*
went forward and offered his penis
to Pan's salivating mouth.
The goat-god did not disdain him,
and began sucking Vitalis, who said
"May this new god have great initiative!"

The head-over-heels, skull-thrown-back
spit-roast of Pan by Antinous and Vitalis
continued until the two young men caught eyes,
smiled, and stopped, withdrawing,
then took each others' hands
and went off to one side,
sitting with arms entwined
in their post-coital bliss.

Hadrian, oddly inspired by what he had just seen,
took his wife by the hand, and lovingly lead her
to Pan's side, where he delicately undressed her
and then himself, placing Pan between their naked bodies.
Pan held Sabina up before him like a champion
while Hadrian penetrated Pan from behind.
In their triple enjoyment, Hadrian shouted
"May this new god act for the people's justice!"
while Sabina, breathless in pleasure, whispered
"May this new god always be loyal to its deepest desires!"

Following the emperor's example,
Trajan and Plotina, like an elderly couple,
with poise and dignity overflowing
where youth and grace would have dwelled earlier,
relieved Hadrian and Sabina of their duties
and assumed their places.
Though joy seemed far from their initial responses,
it soon coursed through them more strongly
than even the most passionate youthful lovers' throes.

The indomitable emperor Trajan proclaimed
"May this new god never be daunted by a challenge!"
as his regal wife Plotina, with decorum, dictated
"May this new god never waver from its goals!"

Ever the imitator of Hadrian,
Herodes likewise took Regilla,
his arm around her shoulder,
and each took their expected positions
before and behind the besotted Pan.
The two simultaneously felt the happiness
of passionate begetting and devoted parenting
as they each gave their blessings:
"May this new god not fear passionate emotions!"
"May this new god never forget its dignity!"

Polydeukion and his two fellow *Trophimoi*
and Regillus, Herodes' young son
perhaps felt the most self-conscious of all,
being youths now performing before all eyes.
What they lacked in experience, however,
was more than made up for in fun and play.
They placed Pan on all fours,
Memnon had sex with him from behind,
Polydeukion penetrated him orally,
and Achilles and Regillus on each side
fucked Pan in his big floppy goat-ears.
"May this god uphold all heroic virtues!"
"May this god's mind be serious!"
"May this god's body be vigorous!"
"May this god's spirit be ever-youthful!"

Hadrian's sister, *Diva* Domitia Paulina, approached the god alone,
like the goddess Selene, drawn by his pastoral simplicity.
Their lovemaking was the picture of tenderness,
the woman as regal as any queen would ever be
in the unpretentious, unadulterated, and sweet
sexual congress of any woman with any man.

"May this god not shun convention when it is beneficial!"

Diva Marciana, elder sister of Trajan, eldest of the group
approached Pan like a longtime husband—
though her body was as vigorous as in her youth,
her decorum and her status, and her own inclination
lead her to treat him like an affectionate companion:
she laid her hand upon his member,
and he put both hands on her breasts,
and in between embraces of the arms and gentle kisses,
Marciana spoke her wishes for the future deity:
"May this god know the simplest pleasures of touch."

The four women who were left—
a *Diva*, a poetess, and two daughters of Herodes—
went forward in pleasant confusion,
impressed but daunted by their predecessor's creativity.
Pan, unbridled in animality, unrestrained in form,
made his tail a second phallus, made his head multiply...

With each of his heads he ate out the sisters Athenais and Elpinike
while Matidia and Julia Balbilla rode him above and below.
"May this god have the love of its children!"
"May this god take satisfaction in its offspring!"
"May this god know the happiness of parenting!"
"May this god know the power of the voice!"

The deified mortals, in an exhausted pile,
simply sat enjoying the exquisite feeling
of satisfied skin against satisfied skin...
but they had forgotten the last of their number
in their gregarious giggling:

Favorinus of Arles, the eunuch orator.
He looked at the group of deified mortals,
shook his head, rolled his eyes, turned up his nose,
then turned his back on them and disrobed.

They struggled to catch a glimpse of him from the front,
but he turned away from their prying eyes each time.
And though they had forgotten him,
Pan would never forget what was about to occur.
The orator's small breasts,
an empty scrotum and small flaccid penis
would not have seemed impressive to many,
and may even have been a cause for derision with some.
How limited is the understanding of too many mortals!

Favorinus set upon Pan like a lion to an antelope,
filling each of his orifices in turn
with his unerect cock, dripping with pre-cum,
and then each of Pan's orifices in turn again,
showering the goat-god with kisses, licks, bites, scratches,
and eliciting from him groans of such deep ecstasy
every other deified mortal present felt inadequate.

One statement from the orator was not enough:

**"May this new deity never be so limited
as to think that flesh has any limits,
that pleasure is only in expelling or receiving,
that any body is either deficient or undeserving,
that eroticism is bounded by genitals and orifices,
that what seems small and lacking in hardness
is in any way diminished in accepting or bestowing pleasure.
And may the words to articulate such things
be easily upon the lips and tongue of this new deity!"**

When Favorinus was finished, he strode away
as proud and haughty as an Olympic victor.
Not another mortal nor god that day
was more desired nor enjoyed by Pan,
nor more lamented for having left Pan's embraces.

Pachrates came forward again.

"Though what has occurred now is divine
and is possessed of sacred and holy power,
the immortal gods will now have their ways
and contribute to the parentage of the new god."

The gods amongst the gods
are not slaves to familiar forms;
they know well that the generation of bodies
even upon the earth does not require sex,
nor even a token observance of physical necessities.
Pan lamented this in comparison to his mortal sex partners,
and the deified mortals, at no point in their eternities,
felt more envious of their former physical existences
than at this time, when the gods' orgy
was a show of masks and lights
in comparison to the skin and flesh extravaganza
that they had enjoyed only moments before.

Osiris and Isis stood on each side of Pan,
their divine essences passing into him without effort.
"If this new god knows death, may it know resurrection."
"May every secret of magic be known to this new god."

Minos, the prosecutor and judge of the dead
approached and spoke his blessing
as his own divine seed passed into Pan.
"May this new god have insight into its ancestors."

A god, a demigod, and a hero came forth:
Dionysos, Herakles, and Achilleus.
**"Though this new god may know clothes not appropriate for it,
may this new god never be in doubt about its gender."**

Vertumnus, god of the shifting seasons,
answered on the tails of the last blessing,
**"But may this new god, likewise,
never fear to wear the clothes
of whatever role may be needed
to accomplish its ends."**

44

The heroine Atalanta, Amazonian woman,
spoke her blessing as her essence joined Pan:
"No matter the clothes or the roles, though,
may this new god never be restrained in its actions."

Selene, goddess of the moon,
came forth to give her blessing:
"May this new god wax and wane,
grow and recede, as it sees fit."

Helen of Sparta and Troy, heroine,
gave her sweet wishes to the developing being:
"May this new god never hesitate
to give up all for its heart's desires."

Euphorion, the blessed child
blasted with Zeus' lightning,
son of Helen and Achilleus
on the island of Ogygia,
winged like an Eros, and as lovely,
came forth to offer his seed:
"May this god never be cursed
nor derided by any previous god."

Thetis, mother of Achilleus,
Bestowed this blessing on the being:
"May this new god have both the strength of lions
but also the cunning of serpents."

Pomona, goddess of fruitfulness, spoke:
"May this new god be fertile
in ways not limited to physical offspring."

Apollon, the Delphic Pythian Phoebus,
in a shower of laurel leaves contributed
both blessing and divine seed to the mix.
"May this new god always heed the voice from within."

Hermes, the guide of souls and gate-keeper,
gave a silver feather into Pan's container.
**"May this new god be a breaker of boundaries,
but also an establisher and defender of new limits."**

Three-faced Hekate, night-flying, raging,
brought her contribution to the god:
**"May this new god be united in itself
where others only see multiplicity."**

Heavenly, man-slaying, Cyprian Aphrodite,
like foam upon waves, added her gifts:
"May this new god inspire desire in others."

The golden-and-turquoise lady of Egypt,
Hathor of the dances and inebriation,
was tired of the disembodiment of the gods
in creating this new god's body;
she came in shaking her sistrum
and had the entire company
stamping and sweating in a circle
for hour upon hour, chanting and squealing
while she relished every moment
of her copulation with Pan as if he were Min.
**"May this new god dance, sing, and intoxicate
with dancing and singing and intoxication!"**

Poseidon came next, like a wave overtaking Pan,
bathing, drenching, saturating every pore:
"May this new god create waves and shatter the earth!"

Twice-visaged Ianus, both old and young,
both male and female, opener and closer, prayed:
"May this new god become expert at endings and beginnings!"

Kastor and Polydeukes, mortal and immortal,
the Dioskouroi twins, conveyed their dual wish:
"May this new god be abundant in both shadows and lights."

Hapi, the ample-breasted god of the Nile,
arrived to inundate the new being with favor:
**"May this new god fructify like a father,
but nurture as a mother."**

Primordial Nyx, goddess mother of the night,
overtook Pan in her engulfing darkness.
"May all potentialities come forth from this new god."

Bright-tressed Iris, divine messenger,
bestowed her rainbow upon Pan.
"May this new god be a beacon of varied hues!"

Four deities then came to the fore:
Allah and his three daughters,
Allat, Manat, and Al-Uzza.
**"May this new god have my mercy and compassion,
and even greater than I have had."**
"May this new god have ferocity of spirit!"
"May this new god know its rightful fate!"
"May this new god have favorable luck!"

Two deities approached Pan
from the tribes of the Israelites
bearing physical parts of themselves to donate.
YHWH, called Iao Sabaoth by the Greeks,
first made his offering:
**"For the foundation of your body,
however it may be, I offer to this new god
my foreskin—may it give pleasure and protection
to you which I never allowed it to give to me."**
Lilith, owl-clawed holy one,
then made her offering:
**"For the foundation of your body,
however it may be, I offer to this new god
my beard—may it be beautiful and warming
and be your glory as equally as it has been my fear."**

A wandering figure in a tattered cloak,
Cynic-like, having given all his possessions away,
approached the scene with curiosity,
and decided to lend his blessing to the effort:
Yeshua, son of Miriam.
"May this new god be unafraid
to make the male into the female,
the female into the male,
the outer into the inner
and the inner into the outer."

 A woman forgotten, but burning bright
with a love and a will, a precious pearl,
Marguerite Porete, came forth to speak.
"May this new god do its work without fear,
no matter what others may say
about the 'falsity' of its gender."

A triad from wildest Thrace
approached the being-in-becoming
to add their blessings to the blood.
Sabazios spoke first: **"Like me,**
may this new being never stint
in becoming whatever it may wish."
Mother Bendis was next to bless.
"May this new being be a parent
to many children, fiercely but gently."
Kotys completed the titan-like triad:
"May the sex and pleasure of that being
be as raucous and regenerative as my rites."

Two Greeks then approached Pan.
Hermaphroditos spoke first:
"May this new god possess both male and female anatomy."
Tiresias spoke second:
"May this new god possess both male and female wisdom."

48

A trio of deities from Asia Minor came.
Cybele, the Magna Mater, bestowed thus:
"May this new god be the mother of all!"
Agdistis, the powerful being, dictated:
"May this new god be whole and holy,
even if others only see a monster."
Attis, arisen but dismembered, decreed:
"May this new god never fear changing its body as necessary!"

An odd pair of deities joined the assembly,
bringing their benedictions to blend into the being:
Loki, the mother of monsters, strife-stirrer, said
"May this new god create chaos where it is most needed!"
while Gwydion, good storyteller, sow and surrogate, spoke
"May this new god put its body against others in love and war freely!"

In a chariot pulled by two magnificent steeds,
with Lóeg mac Ríangabra at the reins,
Cú Chulainn of the Ulaid, son of Lug, came,
leapt from the chariot like a salmon upstream,
and said his words at spear-point:
"May the gods and the non-gods
bless this being, and may my gifts
of boldness, beauty, and derided youth
be this being's own in abundance."

An Egyptian goddess,
said to be two-thirds male
yet still undeniably goddess
strode forth like an arrow surely shot—
Neith, mother of the cosmos:
"May this new deity
enlighten from the darkness,
pouring forth all from the depths."

A being who was sometimes one,
sometimes three, varying
in gender from male to female to male
from far and further in the east
came to appear amidst them:
Avolakiteshvara, the compassionate,
Kuan Yin, the merciful,
Kannon, the expedient.
In a voice sometimes one, sometimes three,
the divine being/s gave this boon:
"May this new god be singular in purpose
even if multiple in form—
consumed with the compassionate release of all sentient beings."

Two beings from India, similar in form
were followed by a third goddess.
The two were like males on the right
but like women on the left:
the goddess cut off her own breasts
though she was still a nurturing mother.
Ardhnarishvara, the first, of Shiva and Parvati,
Hari-Hara the second, of Shiva and Mohini
(who was Vishnu as a woman),
Bahuchara-Mata the third.
Together, the three pronounced their favors,
pouring forth their combined *shakti*—
"May this god defy history, identity, and individuality
to manifest however it may choose."

Three virgin Greek goddesses arrived.
Though virgins, they would become mothers.
But though mothers, they would not pass on
their godly gametes to Pan
even in the metaphysical ways
and discarnate fashions
the other gods had done.

First, Hestia, fire of the hearth
burned like a bright torch
penetrating Pan's eyes, passing her power
and essence into the new being.
"May this new god have every power of my fire."

Second, Pallas Athena, owl-eyed,
aegis-bearing, spoke her words
into Pan's ears, transmitting
her parentage into the new being.
"May this new god have all of my wisdom."

Thirdly, Artemis the maiden huntress,
of Brauron and Ephesus, Diana of Nemi,
upright, indomitable, never ruled by male,
drew forth from her left breast
a handful of her own heart's-blood,
rammed it down Pan's throat
without permission nor apology
to mingle with the previous ingredients.
"Though I have not given birth to it,
though I will never give birth to it,
may every god and mortal know this well:
I am the mother of this new god
and all its offspring forever after,
my blood is its blood, my mysteries its mysteries,
my power its power, no matter what any may say."

Gods and deified mortals alike
were awe-struck with these final gifts;
it was assumed that all had been completed.

Pachrates was about to speak,
when from the ground beneath and air above
two coiling figures converged, green and purple,
meeting in a flash of fiery sparks and lightning,
and bathed in a soft white glow
the goddess Ananke, unavoidable necessity,
manifested before the company.

"Gods and heroes, justified dead,
this business of yours pleases me.
**This new god is needed now, more than ever,
and therefore necessity will also be its mother.**
But one contribution remains to be given."

A near-forgotten god, elderly, dressed as a farmer,
came into the company carrying a dark clod.
He went to Pan, who sat expectantly,
ready for whatever this god might do.

With fist closed tightly around the clod,
the god thrust his forearm into Pan's anus,
placed his load within him, and withdrew.

"I, Sterculinus, give the final blessing.
This god and its offspring will know, alas,
no end of scorn and disdain, abuse,
and will be given every kind of shit.
**May this new god, with my blessing,
be able to turn every kind of shit it is given
into the most pure and productive fertilizer,
so that even a millionth of it
makes this god's fields abundant beyond measure."**

The work of the gods was done—
the divine embryo had been created
and now needed to be carried to term.

IV.

The many gods began dispersing back to their realms,
leaving a small band of their number there,
the deified mortals still in awe over the process.

Pachrates, unfazed, continued on.
"Pan cannot hold the divine embryo for long.
If it is not removed from him, it will overwhelm him."

Pan removed one of his curled ram-horns from his head,
turning it upright like a ready libation-cup.
The ambrosial liquid of the divine essences
swirled and shimmered, nearly overflowing its edges.

Pan could not hold the turbulent vessel, however,
and so Hermes summoned two divine serpents,
Glykon and Chnoubis, to coil themselves
around the horn to guard it and hold it.

"But who shall give birth to this being?"
Antinous asked in astonishment.

"Few beings are powerful enough
even to attempt it, I'm afraid."

Pachrates suggested, "What of the sky-goddess Nut?"

Hermes replied, "No, her womb is full nightly
with each day's rebirth of the Barque of Re."

Favorinus interjected, "And, it seems to me
that an ordinary birth from a female
is unwarranted and not suited to this new god."

"Agreed," Ananke announced.
"An unconventional gestation is required."

"But who, short of Zeus, could carry this out?"
Herodes Attikos posed the question candidly.

"Few, if any," both Dionysos and Athena agreed.

"Then, it's settled: I shall notify father,
and he will come here immediately to see to this,"
Hermes declared and disappeared from the company.

The serpents coiled tightly, but could not move,
nor could any deity present hope to heft the horn.
They all assumed it would be safe in the scales
of lion-maned Chnoubis and horse-haired Glykon.

One by one and two by two, those remaining left,
while the ambrosial nectar coalesced and coagulated,
quickening into a liquid being,
not fully formed, not fully defined.

But moments passed, and became hours,
and hours days, and days months...
though in the divine realms,
time has little meaning and no substance.

Someone had to re-set the clocks, however,
so that the passing years seemed as seconds
to Zeus and the other gods.

And though Glykon and Chnoubis writhed
but did not move an inch to either side,
the ground beneath them was moved,
as was the sphere of the horizon surrounding them.

One goddess was responsible for this,
one being devoted to chaos and discord,
one power that planned to ruin plans,
one personality who always keeps things interesting.

Early night fell on horizon and shifted earth;
Reeling eyelids of snakes became heavier and heavier;
Insatiable thirst was kindled in a far-off throat;
So, a golden apple fell into the divine embryo.

V.

The night had been dark, but the sun was rising.

Set emerged, his ears like sturgeon's fins cutting through water
sliced the arid air in the early moments of dawn.
It had been a difficult night, and sleep would be welcome.

But he stumbled and strayed, for a place had not been made for him.

From out of Egypt's deserts he meandered, looking for shelter.

He did not find it, and instead collapsed, nose in the sand.

He slept the sleep only the dead who are just know.
He dreamt dreams only the assured and enlightened enjoy.
He rested in a restfulness only the honest laborer contemplates.

From rest, he stirred to dreams; from dreams, he shifted to sleep;
from sleep, he rose to twilight thoughts; from thoughts, he awoke.

He was parched in the desert and needed to drink.

He moved one leg, like a pillar, to stand like a mountain;
he opened one eye, like a serpent, watchful on the horizon;
he stretched out one strong, red arm from Egypt's wastelands.

The Nile had not inundated for decades.

Across the furthest reaches of the *Amduat*, his arm extended.
Across the span of the fixed stars his other arm groped.

His fingers fixed around an object, a tuft of hair.
He pulled his right arm back before his face.
The forelock on the bald head of Kairos was in his grasp.

"You are not water; you are not beer.
Even if you were urine, I would drink you,
but you are only a bald naked boy with wings."

"I am a herald who has come forth knocking."

"Say your piece and be done with me,
or I will crack your skull for my wine goblet."

"Feel the lights of the Milky Way with your left hand.
There you will find the opportunity you seek."

Set loosened his grasp for but a second's fraction,
the bald naked boy with wings disappeared.

His thirst was a dry river weeping dust.

His left hand felt a refreshing cold,
a hint of moisture, an aura of liquidity.
His nose drew him onwards to its source.

An upturned horn full of liquid stood
guarded by two coiled serpents,
one green and maned, one orange and lion-headed.

His spear like a shaft of shooting starlight appeared.

Though Chnoubis is no Apophis,
though Glykon is no Apep,
both feared the spear and fled.
The upturned horn remained, unmoved.

Set seized the horn and drank, deeply.

VI.

Set was asleep, his hand still gripping the horn,
when the company of the deified mortals found him.

Not a drop of the divine liquid was left for Zeus.

Even then, something was stirring within Set.

Trajan and Hadrian were worried, Antinous uneasy,
but Lucius Marius Vitalis was confident.
"He gave birth to a child of Horus before;
surely he will be able to bear this new god!"

Set awoke immediately, stroked Vitalis' hair,
and asked for another drink.

Herodes Attikos and Favorinus tried to explain
in the most pacific terms possible what had happened.
Set stood up, as if about to rage like a thrashing crocodile,
but instead he only said the following:

"I have been the bearer of a god's seed before
without having the pleasure of receiving it directly.
I can do so again, but I insist
that since I will be performing this benefit,
I have the pleasure I was previously denied—
I do not mean the child Horus,
I mean this youth, Lucius Marius Vitalis."

Hadrian and Antinous seemed horrified for a moment,
but Vitalis was calm. "I will do this."
The others left them in peace
while Set and Vitalis sipped enjoyment
from one another's bodies at every limb and orifice.

It was then the enormity of the task
and of the divine offspring within him
hit Set like a tsunami against the shore.

"My boy, what will happen?
This thing within me searches for its place,
it does not find it within my divine organs...
it is powerful, and could tear me apart.
If it does, I cannot defend the Solar Barque of Re,
and the sun will not rise,
and even the gods cannot withstand such a state."

"Your burden will last no more than three days—
each day will feel like three months, two hours like a week,
but your strength will remain with you
until the moment the birth shall occur.
Just like with Horus' child before,
you shall open your mouth
and speak the new being into existence.
The best midwives will be found for you
and you will return to your duties soon after delivery.
The child will be born when the sun
is safely in the sky overhead at noon."

"You are a wise and pleasing youth,
and I have had my enjoyment from you.
Please take your own contentment with me
as if you were Min of Coptos and I Hathor."

"But Hathor has a vagina!"

"Come now, naïve boy—
even Horus comes into his house
by the back entrance occasionally!"

Vitalis was never more eager nor erect
on that occasion when he ploughed Set's furrow.
The divine child within the red god's guts
felt this draw from without, this added energy...
and though Ananke could not have foreseen it,
she did not oppose what happened as a result.

Dusk came, and dawn followed—the first day.

The morning arrived, and Set was rotund,
gravid with the wombless burden he would bear.
He sweated, craved unusual foods,
and was unable to stand.
Vitalis laid Set's head in his lap,
stroked his ears and hair,
and kissed his scalp.

Two visitors came calling
from far away in the east.

The first seemed blue-skinned and wild-eyed,
screaming and disheveled, tongue lolling,
teeth dripping blood, fingernails gore-stained...
but only if viewed from thought of loss—
otherwise, she was a gentle, smiling, white-clad matron.

The second was a champion of a figure,
now a towering giant, now a diminutive creature,
a tail spanning light years or inches,
a mouth that could swallow the sun,
legs for leaping from Lanka to Saturn,
and carrying a mace in one hand
and a mountain in the other.

The two were welcomed by Vitalis,
even though Set shut his eyes in his unease.
They came bearing blessings.

Kali spoke first.
"Though I was not a part
of this god's begetting,
I will be his mother, or her mother,
no matter what the case may be.
And, like myself, where some may fear this god's visage
in truth, only liberation and bliss will come from seeing it."

Set opened his eyes, nodded wordlessly,
and closed them again.
Vitalis expressed his thanks
for this unusual, unexpected *darshan*.

Hanuman, the divine monkey,
came forward and prostrated before Set.
"Though I have a son, strangely engendered,
and my own birth involved many parents,
in my life I came to have another mother—Sita.
May I, too, therefore, be as a father to this god,
as I am this god's son and devotee.
May what cannot be accomplished
through courtesy and communication
be within the reach of this god's power.
"And one other gift I have to give,
Useless among gods though many think it is:
Modesty.

"For even at my birth, I was clad,
and my loins were girded and concealed
from prying eyes by this red *langoti*—
even thus, may this god be born,
and may none not wished by this god
know what may be concealed beneath."

Set opened his eyes, nodded wordlessly,
and closed them again.
Vitalis, confused, expressed his thanks,
and thought of days passed in *gymnasia*,
the pleasures of sight and touch
in baths and beds and *palaestra* grounds,
and he could not imagine any of these
with the intervention of a stitch of clothing.

Dusk came, and dawn followed—the second day.

Set rose on the morn, stretched to breaking point,
and Vitalis did all he could to make him comfortable.

Embassies of gods arrived from everywhere,
but he only admitted the first: Coyote.
The strange creature sniffed, and giggled,
and brushed his fur against the god's trunk,
and with a gleam in his eyes and smiling teeth,
he licked him and scurried away.
And for a moment, Set opened his eyes,
and smiled, and laughed,
his discomfort departed for a few seconds.

Thoth was tasked with recording the gifts
that the many gods were bringing,
every blessing, every boon,
every spell and incantation.

As the night drew near, and the line of visitors
did not diminish from horizon to horizon
the time for Set's confinement approached.
Into the small house with Set and Vitalis
were admitted a limited number of deities:
the four wives of Set—
Nephthys, Neith, Astarte, and Anat—
and his two sons—Sobek and Anubis;
four midwives from the Greeks and Egypt—
Eilitheia, Artemis, Taweret and Heqet;
and over the house Selket stood guard.
Gwydion and Loki, males who had given birth,
were there to see their new child.
Two more Greeks joined the group:
Hephaistos, to lend his hammer to the effort if needed,
and Zeus, who was there—so he said—
mostly for moral support.

Antinous, the first father,
also came to welcome the new god.

Finally, Horus was admitted to witness the birth.

Dusk came, and dawn followed—the third day.

VII.

But after such a difficult process—
of unconventional pregnancy,
of entirely novel begetting—
what followed seemed easy in comparison.

An hour before noon arrived,
the swollen belly of Set began stirring,
first in one direction, then another,
first swirling clockwise, then counter,
shifting to the right, then the left,
then up, then down.

Artemis and Eilitheia held his arms,
and Heqet and Taweret held his legs,
while Vitalis cradled his head...
but in truth, none knew what would happen
nor what to expect in this situation.

Hephaistos, soot-stained, stood ready
with his hammer raised to rend flesh
and break bone, of belly or of skull,
and Zeus had lightning prepared to flash
if for illumination or destruction it was necessary.

But as Re's Celestial Barque reached its exaltation
and its pinnacle in the sky above was attained,
a sound came.
It was like a low grumbling at first,
and those there thought it was Set groaning,
but they were mistaken, for it came from within.
A single birth-pang struck, knocking Set over,
and the four goddesses lost their grip on his limbs.
But, glowing now like a lantern,
Set rose to his feet.

Set stretched his neck and raised his head,
spread out his arms overhead, as if in prayer,
and opened his mouth.
Light like the rays of the sun
streamed forth from his throat,
and a thousand times a thousand voices
in chorus like a chord from the celestial spheres
sounding together at once
gained in volume as the light was eclipsed
and one word with the breath from within him
was formed: *psyche*, "soul."

And with neither blood nor pain that was visible,
a bright goddess came forth from his mouth fully formed.

Her hair cascaded in a gentle wave
over her thin shoulders,
and her small breasts emerged into view
before her muscled slim abdomen;
but as her slightly widened hips came forth
the assembled deities were astonished,
for just as Hanuman had stated,
the goddess wore a covering around her waist
that concealed whatever was between her legs,
now emerging, ending the length of her body.

It was as if the wings of an eagle were in her shadow.

She stood on her own, spotless and sparkling,
and with a rich voice she spoke:
"I am Panpsyche."

Zeus, father of gods and humans,
saw this beautiful goddess
and went toward her, embraced her,
and put his hand immediately on her pubic mound,
but then stood back in confusion.

"You have neither asked permission
nor been granted it, Olympian!"
the goddess stated sharply in reply.
Zeus, rejected, began to be angry in response,
his thunder fulminating in his hand,
when Set tapped him on the shoulder.
"Do it, and what Typhon did with your sinews
will seem like the best blow-job you ever had."

Zeus, unhappy at this turn of events,
stood back, but did not speak nor act further.

Antinous came forth and embraced his daughter,
and clad a saffron *chiton* around her shoulders.

And as Neith and Artemis also welcomed their new daughter,
Vitalis cried out:
"Wait! This birth is not yet complete!
There is more!"

All observed how still Set was rounded,
but where the motions to the right had ceased,
the left, counter-clockwise swirling continued,
and a high-pitched cry seemed to erupt from inside him.

All prepared to receive another child
who would be spoken into existence from Set's mouth,
but not a one among them expected what occurred.

The high-pitched cry lowered, and lowered,
and became a deep and guttural groan,
and Set's entrails twisted within him.
Without sound, without shit,
but with pain that would not be fathomed,
Set, standing, birthed another from his anus.

The feet emerged first, soles ready
to stand upon solid ground as soon as it was touched.
The knees were seen, worn and calloused
from years of work and play and strain.
But, like his sister, the thin waist emerged
covered, the genitals concealed from view,
as the torso slid out of Set's body.
Scars could be seen on the god's chest,
and when his head and arms appeared at last
he was a virtual twin to his sister, save
with short-cropped hair and a bit of stubble.

The shadow of a bull's horns were on his head.

**"I am Panhyle, and it is no small matter
that I was not expected among you."**

Zeus saw in him a second Ganymede,
and a Zagreus of the new era,
but being unrelated to him,
he went toward him, intent
on snatching him away to Hera's spite and envy.
But, when in Greek tradition
he reached to fondle the young god's genitals
he again retreated in confusion
at what he felt beneath the folds.

"You have neither asked permission
nor been granted it, Olympian!"
the god spat stingingly in response.

But this time, Zeus knew better
than to react as he did before
with the unburdened Set at his back.

Antinous came forward and kissed his son,
put a *chlamys* around his shoulders,
and Neith and Artemis embraced him as well.

Panhyle turned to Lucius Marius Vitalis
and spoke to him:
"Father, you paved the way
for my birth and emergence from father Set.
To you, I owe my life!"
Vitalis embraced his son with tears,
but confusion reigned in his heart.

Panhyle spoke to his sister, squinting:
"Why did you not speak of me to them?"
Panpsyche answered his question candidly, bitterly:
"I knew you'd come forward
whether I said anything or not,
there was nothing I could do about it."

Panhyle was angry.
"I could have torn our father apart from the inside!"
Panpsyche was disdainful.
"Like I couldn't have just as easily?
But I found a way to come forth
without being tainted by the body's limits."

The two were in enmity with each other
before they were on the earth even a moment.

Antinous tried to calm them down.
"My children, my daughter and son!
You have pleased your many parents
even by your mere existence—
surely you can manage to have peace between you?"

Vitalis put himself between them,
touched the shoulder of one, then another,
and tried to move them toward each other.

Before they could touch,
Panpsyche screeched
and Panhyle grunted,
and they turned from each other
and stepped away.

VIII.

The sons of Set, Sobek and Anubis,
as well as Hephaistos with his hammer and Horus
and even Zeus—hopeful and undaunted
that he might convince the youth otherwise one day—
took Panhyle into their company
and departed from the house.
Minos, Dionysos, and Poseidon
met them at the door
and ambled away with him.

Panpsyche, not content to leave on foot
rose into the air, and like rays of sun and moon,
Astarte, Anat, Artemis, Neith, and Nephthys
left with Panpsyche in their midst,
joined above the house
by Hathor and Isis, Lilith and Selene.

Eilitheia and Heqet and Taweret,
their work—which was not work—done,
set off for their own destinations.

Loki looked at Gwydion, who looked back,
and said, briefly, "This will make a good story."
The two departed, amused and uncertain.

Antinous, Vitalis, and Set
remained in the house, the divinized dismayed,
the godly confounded.
Set took his spear in hand,
spoke of the coming evening's activities
when Apophis would again be slain,
and added, "But hours remain until then.
Stay if you wish, Antinous,
but I would like to fuck more first,
so unless you plan on joining in,
I would suggest you leave now, if you please."

Antinous was intrigued by the offer,
but thought better of it
and instead went to tell the others
of the two births that had just transpired.

Over the course of the days that came,
Panpsyche met all her mothers, fathers, and parents,
thanked them for her essence and character,
and departed in a wind of words.
Panhyle came into the presence of his many parents,
thanked them for making him what he was,
kissed their feet and touched the earth beneath them,
and then went his own way striding.
The brother and sister never crossed paths,
never inquired after one another,
never smiled nor commented when one parent
mentioned the other twin sibling in passing.
Apollon and Artemis, Kastor and Polydeukes
all found this situation stupefying, intolerable.

But one parent who saw more of them
than any other amongst god-born and deified
was Favorinus of Arles, the eunuch orator.

Panpsyche came to him, spoke of his influence,
discussed her ideas and experiences with him,
and even engaged in heated but loving debate,
then always showered him with praise and appreciation
before taking the orator's leave in a flutter of speech.

Panhyle always seemed to arrive
when his sister had recently vacated,
and though he and the orator exchanged words
and expressed the deepest filial affections,
mostly he just sat with him, hand in hand,
or embraced him, sitting on his lap
clasped together, content, wordless.

And if one asked either of the siblings
who understood them more than any other,
both would have answered "Father Favorinus"
without doubt nor hesitation.

It wasn't until years later that their paths crossed.

They had asked their mothers, Athena and Artemis,
where the most secluded, concealed clear pool
for bathing in the wilderness happened to be.
And though their mother Aphrodite offered the use of her spring
to sustain youth and increase beauty,
her two children declined, wishing only privacy.

Tiresias, their father, remembered the way to the pool,
and showed it to each of them on different occasions,
recalling his last sight within the pool...
he wiped away the tears that came
because such touching beauty is blinding.

The pool was a wide expanse,
a calm secluded backwater of the Sangarius River.

On a night when their mother Nyx
overshadowed their mother Selene
and their mother Hekate was afoot in the world,
the two came by two different paths
to two ends of the pool.

Separately, but in unison, unknowing
the two slipped out of their modest coverings,
washed them in the river's water
and hung them on bushes to dry.
Though both did not like their nude reflections
in the clear mirror waters on the pool's surface
each felt unburdened and free for a moment,
and entered the pool to bathe.
Neither looked down at their reflections
until the night-dark water submerged their waists
and the gentle current washed their nether-parts
in a pleasurable, sensuous cleansing.

Each reclined in the water, letting go
of all worries and cares, detritus of expectation
rinsing away like dust on glass beneath rainfall.

For that moment of contentment and pleasure
Panhyle felt as if what was below
matched what he knew he was from birth;
for that moment of clear realization
Panpsyche thought as if what was below
was consonant with her most essential nature.

Both felt an accord in mind and body,
soul and matter, identity and physicality
which had been strangely lacking before.

And when their hands descended to their groins
they felt a new presence, a variant shape...
both inhaled in surprise, a high whistle, a low groan—
and turned to see one another.

74

But, what they saw, they misunderstood,
for Panpsyche felt she looked in the mirror
at the stubbled face and dangling penis of herself,
and Panhyle thought he looked in the mirror
at the swelled breasts and lipped vulva of himself,
and both cried out in anguish and disgust,
not realizing that it was not a mirror
into which each of them was peering
but instead another person—their non-identical twin.
The two were a reverse Narcissus,
ignorant not of singularity, but of difference.

And, some say that when this occurred,
Narcissus himself was sitting nearby,
heard the sound and glanced upward
at the twins' reflections in the pool
for the briefest of fleeing moments,
and as his eyes moved back to his own reflection
staring back into his own face,
he stopped again briefly, seeing his visage
reflected, looking elsewhere, for just a moment.

When he resumed his vigil of self-staring
he did not hear the visage-turned-figure
rise up from the reflection of the waters,
walking to the opposite bank of the river
and beginning her own self-gazing practice—Narcissa.

Panpsyche waded, sloshing clumsily
back to her drying garments,
Panhyle sometimes skimmed, sometimes skipped
across the surface to his bushy dresser.
Both were horrified to find
their clothes had been stolen...
what tasteless prank was this?

Fauna had stolen Panhyle's trunks,
wishing to extort lust's favors from him.

Faunus absconded with Panpsyche's panties
intent on ravishing her forcefully.

But neither was below
what they had seemed above
now that their spell of serenity
had been broken and disrupted
by confused visions and lack of reflection.

Faunus gazed on the smooth skin
of Panpsyche's face, her pert breasts,
and when he looked down, licking his lips
only to see Panpsyche's penis displayed
the shock and horror was as great
as Pan's when he mistook Herakles for Omphale
and yet even more—an Actaeon caught out,
a hunter now become the hunted.

He shrieked, and as he did so
every hair from his body dropped from him
and his priapic phallus shriveled so small
it withdrew into him and never again emerged—
he grew breasts and long hair on the spot
and became Fauna, fleeing in fear,
forever cursing all men to never speak
her new name, instead calling her "Bona Dea"
to propitiate her wrath and resentment.

Fauna looked upon the bearded jaw,
the hairy chest and its downward trail
following it until it widened to the mass of hair
arrayed around Panhyle's perfect vulva,
but for this surprise she had no words
and began speaking sentences of gibberish;
her breasts reduced, hair sprouted all over,
and what was inside reverted to outside,
her vagina became a penis, her labia closed to a scrotum,
and her ovaries dropped painfully into testicles.

She was no longer herself any more,
for her vision earned her a reversal of gender,
and in fear and panic she fled into the woods,
forever after being the wild-man Faunus,
who would have the reputation of unrestrained insanity,
the thwarting of successful fertility,
and speaking with strange voices and words.

Panpsyche and Panhyle recovered their clothes,
dressed hastily, and each thought briefly
to glance over their shoulders
to pay one last longing look
at their sibling—beautiful, naked,
as they were or should have been
now wracked with fear, loathing, and remorse,
and each even longed to comfort the other
in ways that each now knew
could be done in fullness of trust
and complementarity of understanding
that not even Favorinus could possess,
but both were too ashamed
at the revelations they had shown
and the apocalypses they had seen—
but, knowing the dangers of mother Hekate's dark night,
they dared not look back, but fled instead.

Panhyle visited his fathers—
Trajan, Hadrian, Antinous, Herodes Attikos,
Polydeukion, Memnon, Achilles, and Regillus—
and with them he learned
the ways of hunting and stalking prey,
of carrying spears and wielding swords,
chariot-driving and horse-riding,
wrestling and throwing the discus.
Then he took turns between these lessons
to learn speech, rhetoric, and writing
from his fathers Favorinus and Lucius Marius Vitalis.

Panpsyche spent time with her mothers—
Plotina, Sabina, Julia Balbilla,
Regilla, Athenais, Elpinike,
Matidia, Marciana, Domitia Paulina,
and Marguerite Porete—
and with them she came to know
every art of speech and poetry,
of singing and lyre-playing,
of philosophical discourse and rhetorical writing,
of weaving and gardening and cooking.
And when she had enough of words
she spent time running in the forest
with her mothers Atalanta and Artemis.

But, there were some satyrs
who were rude to Panhyle,
who would not let him run with them
when they planned phallic processions;
and likewise there were nymphs
who treated Panpsyche poorly,
saying she did not know their mysteries
when three moon goddesses were her mothers.

And at night, she wept;
and through the day, he wept.

Each in turn came to their father Set
as he stood watch in the prow of the Barque of Re.
They plied him with questions,
they complained of their state,
they expressed their common griefs at exclusion.

Each time his children came,
executed like a flawless scripted performance,
Set nodded, and closed his eyes,
and after a time, said, "Silence!"

And when he had made of his children
a male and a female Harpocrates
with his finger held to their lips,
he turned with a flourish of his spear
and drove its point through Apophis' skull,
the serpent of chaos crumbling in a coil,
dead for the moment, but soon to regenerate
when its wriggling, convulsing tail
found its way into the slack open jaws
where poisonous fangs sharp as spikes
would revive its length with the vigor
of a million years of bile and spite.

Set then spoke to each,
"You think I don't know your suffering?
Have I not been rejected of the gods?
Am I not reviled and disrespected,
feared and hated and cursed?
But, only I can carry out this task,
only I can slay Apophis nightly,
only I can wield the power to do this.
The gods tolerate me, they do not
appreciate, nor do they thank,
but it is only because of me
that they are able to exist.
In time, you will be like me—
you will give birth, and have offspring
and you yourselves, by doing this,
will be able to make the sun come up."

"But until then, what will I do?"
Each child's question was the mirror of the other's.

"If there is someone you want killed,
tell me, and it shall be done."

Neither Panpsyche nor Panhyle liked that thought,
but their own rage and disappointment certainly thought it.

Neither Panhyle nor Panpsyche saw the other,
still holding fear and embarrassment too close
under the silt and film of rejection,
never returning to the pool of the Sangarius.

It was then that a challenge
was presented to the divine and deified.

Typhon and Echidna, it was said,
engendered a horrible hippopotamus
that was ravaging up and down the Nile,
destroying villages, killing children,
trampling mothers with babes in arms,
drowning the human hunters who pursued it.
The prayers came to the ears
of all the gods of Egypt
and all those enthroned with the gods of Egypt
and all the children of the gods of Egypt.

Panpsyche heard the prayers of every mother and daughter.
Panhyle heard the prayers of every father and son.

The gods of Egypt came together
to hear the declaration,
the call to arms, the call to the hunt.
Thoth, the ibis-headed scribe,
read the pronouncement to all.

"On behalf of the people of the Two Lands,
the children of Horus and the offspring of Set,
the gods and goddesses of Egypt are called
to rid the land of the plague upon it.
For firstborn sons are stillborn,
and firstborn daughters die in their cradles;
the youngest children expire in youth,
and middle children die in young adulthood.
Fathers die in fear when they see the beast coming,
and mothers die defending their children.

"Therefore, the gods and goddesses are entreated
to rid the Black Land of this beast
by whatever means necessary—
with one condition
imposed by the beast itself:
no spear may harm the creature
which is not thrown by a mother,
nor may any arrow pierce its flesh
that was not fired by a father.
This is the will of the gods."

Hapi, breasted though begetter,
took his weapons and fastened them on;
Neith, two-thirds male but mother,
arrayed her armor about her.
Set and Antinous set their adamant spears
and all the other gods of Egypt
arranged themselves into hunting cohorts.
The Greek gods, the Roman gods,
the Phoenicians and the Judeans,
the Asians and the Gaulish,
the Thracian and the British,
the Germanic and the Indian,
and many more besides
came to join the hunting party.

Panpsyche was on one end of the throng,
Panhyle lingered on the opposite verge.

Thoth spoke: "It is not permitted
for the newest daughter and son of Set
to take part in this hunt—
for the daughter is not a mother,
nor is the son yet a father."

Antinous objected to their exclusion,
as did all their parents in turn.

But Thoth spoke further:
"It is not I, nor the gods,
who have set this limitation,
but the beast itself.
A spear thrown by woman who is not mother
will not wound nor worry the beast;
an arrow fired by man who is not father
will fail and falter in piercing its skin.
I have no power to change the nature
of this beast, only to speak what is there."

The gods and goddesses were used to such *gessi*
and shrugged, stumbling away to their task.
Antinous lingered behind a moment
and tried to console his two children.
He had no words for them,
and so much time had passed for him
since he had been childless and in their position
that he could not give them the advice
that he and Polydeukion and Favorinus
had come up with in their earlier situation.

He wept with them, he embraced each,
and refused to take part in the hunt.
And when Maahes cajoled and called him a coward,
Antinous gave him a smack with his spear-butt
that left him smarting for centuries.

Panpsyche and Panhyle, spears lowered,
looked at each other and said no words,
turning in silence, blessed by Angerona,
wanting to console one another
in their mutual exclusion,
but neither had the words to do so.

Each of the two deities
wandered long and lonely
through desert wastes and dense wilderness,
across harsh moors and heaving mountains.
The hunt like a hundred swarms of bees,
like a spattered spate of tornadoes,
tore through land after land,
country after country,
territory after territory,
but could catch no sign of the beast,
no trail of the terror—
and the dead, and the dying
continued to increase all the while.

The cries and the wails of anguish,
the prayers and the curses of desperation
sounded and reached the ears of the gods
who were deafened by the despair—
Panpsyche and Panhyle heard every one.

When she could stand it no more,
her spear-point became sharp and silver,
and Panpsyche leapt in the direction
she thought the beast might be.

When he could take it no longer,
his arrows became gleaming and gold,
and Panhyle trudged toward the way
he felt the beast might be.

In a corner of southeastern Asia
Panpsyche caught sight of the beast,
glimpsed it as it sped out of view,
its mud-covered rump mocking;
she was given good hospitality there
and departed, bestowing blessings.

On an island in the Caribbean
Panhyle tracked the creature,
was blindsided and nearly trampled by it,
its maw contorted in a devious grin;
he was given a fitting reception there
and departed, granting boons.

She saw it and struck,
it squealed and bled, but got away;
he saw it and attacked,
it grunted, wounded, then escaped.

The hunting parties of the gods
filled with fathers, made up of mothers
neither saw the beast
nor wounded it.

At last, in North America,
Panpsyche tracked the creature
and Panhyle tailed it tirelessly—
a shadow was pursued,
a rustling in the bushes,
a set of footprints,
a trail of terror...
and, at last, the two
ran into each other, literally,
as Coyote cackled and sped away.

Panpsyche dusted herself off,
Panhyle picked himself up;
they finally acknowledged each other,
apologized for their accidental collision,
and, at last,
embraced each other in tears.

In a single glance, Panpsyche
conveyed all the words of her thoughts
over the years since their birth,
since their bath, since the hunt began,
and in another glance, and a gentle touch,
Panhyle echoed back every word and thought.

With a hand on a shoulder, Panhyle
communicated all the emotions felt
since their birth, since their bath,
since the hunt began those years before,
and with another hand, and a knowing nod,
Panpsyche reciprocated every feeling and emotion.

And then, in full understanding,
appreciation, respect, and mutuality,
the twin siblings became inseparable,
and loved each other like Apollon and Artemis,
like Kastor and Polydeukes;
and for the first time in their lives,
and never known in their parents' presence,
in this complete and total comprehension...
they talked about the weather,
about what they liked and looked forward to,
and about every other aspect of life
which no interactions in their existence
had hitherto allowed them to do...
and it was beautifully extraordinary,
and utterly mundane and silly,
and both enjoyed it as nothing ever before.

For a while they wandered and ambled,
sauntered and strolled,
rambled and roved,
until eventually they recalled
the task, the hunt, the beast
that was still killing in droves.

Panpsyche flew above
while Panhyle paced below,
and night became day, days became week,
weeks became month, months became year,
and at last they followed the beast's trail
to the pool of the Sangarius River.

What had once been peaceful and placid
was now sundered and squalid—
the place was a mess,
and the siblings were determined
to restore its beauty
and slay the monster at last.

Laying down a distraction,
Panhyle fired five, fifteen, fifty arrows
impaling the feet, piercing the eyelids,
perforating the skull of the beast.
It unhinged its jaw
and bellowed, bellicose, back at the archer.

But then, from above, Panpsyche struck.
She stabbed with her spear
first through the skull,
then, retracting, thrust again
through the heart, bursting it
and leaving the beast a bloody pile.

It was not dead yet.

As its life dwindled away
with each drop of blood spilled
it thrashed about, tossing Panpsyche
from her aerial vantage point
to the sodden ground beneath.
Enraged, Panhyle sprang forward
to his sister's defense, slashing
with a sword his father Set had given.

The beast bit with its teeth
and trampled with its feet,
but eventually, when the last of its blood
drained away from its wounds,
it fell down, dead, never to revive.

Panhyle and Panpsyche were gravely wounded.
The blood of the beast was ground into the mud,
but the Sangarius River flowed red
with the blood of brother and sister.
They cried out in their pain
and the hunting parties of the gods
knew the brother who was not a father
and the sister who was not a mother
had been victorious in their hunt,
but had been mortally wounded.

Antinous was the first to arrive,
ready to slay whoever would disturb them.
The other gods who were their parents
and goddesses who had brought them to birth
assembled slowly, sadly,
offering them every succor
as they lay dying.

Asklepios, Imhotep, and Miach
had arrived too late.

IX.

A funeral party was made
from the hunting party,
and Anubis and Wepwawet
were called to convey the couple
to their place in the underworld.

As Anubis tried to strip their bodies
of what little clothing they wore,
Antinous stopped him and refused
to let any god uncover their nakedness.
They could not go into the *Duat*.

Ishtar and Tammuz suggested
they might go into Irkalla;
Ereshkigal and Nergal agreed.

As each of the seven gates of Irkalla
were reached and surpassed,
more and more of the gods drifted away
from the ranks of the funeral party.
When the last gate was passed
only Antinous remained carrying their bodies.

He wept bitterly and lengthily
when he reached the depths of Irkalla,
his tears were equal to the ocean
that had been shed for him,
for Hephaistion, for Hylas, for Hyakinthos,
for Patroklos, for Enkidu, for Jonathan,
for Fer Diad, for Kallisto, for Krokus,
for all those slain unjustly on the earth,
and in recompense for the many
for whom no tears were shed
nor whose names were remembered.

At last, when he had wept for a century,
Antinous came forth once more,
the doorkeepers of Irkalla yielding before him
and speaking their praises of him as he passed.
He returned, and mourned
with all the parents of Panpsyche and Panhyle.

But one was not content merely to mourn:
Favorinus of Arles.
He spoke to Avolakiteshvara,
who spoke to Kuan Yin, who spoke to Kannon,
who spoke to Hapi, who spoke to Neith,
who spoke to Yeshua, who spoke to Allat...
and, a plan was born.

Dionysos, Herakles, and Hermes
would all go down to Irkalla
and bring Panpsyche and Panhyle back.

And when they passed the seven gates
and came into the presence of Ereshkigal
and her husband Nergal,
they asked for the bodies of their children.
These were granted to them.
Dionysos carried Panpsyche,
Herakles carried Panhyle
and Hermes made sure the gates opened before them.

They walked, then they ran,
then they flew, then they sped—
for behind them, every dread thing
that Irkalla could muster
revolted against the loss
of the two divine bodies—
but the three never looked back.

They returned to the middle worlds,
they laid the lifeless bodies down
and, seeing them still dead,
they wept again.
Slowly, their many divine parents
gathered and brought their tears
to pool with those shed before.
An ocean equal to Antinous' century
was formed before too long.
And this time, their cries and keening
did not go unanswered, neither
were their tears wasted nor useless.

From a place which was no place
Kurgarru and Kalaturru emerged,
alighting at the place of mourning.
From the ocean of tears
they made the waters of life
in a measure thirty times thirty.
From the dust of desolation
they made the bread of life
in a measure sixty times sixty.
From the sounds of sadness
they made the fire of life
in a measure ninety times ninety.
From their own souls
they breathed the breath of life:
Panpsyche and Panhyle arose.

The jubilation that the group of gods
expressed was like the echo of creation,
and the world was made anew again
with the ecstasy and the excitement
of the first shout of pleasure
sounded across the cosmos.

Panhyle and Panpsyche took it in turns
to weave the tale of their reunion,
to tell all present of their test
and how they had slain the beast.

Taweret, hippopotamus goddess of Egypt,
giver of safe delivery in childbirth,
nodded approvingly from the back.

And as the two saw her do this,
suddenly they realized
they had children aplenty—
children who were daughters and sons
born between organs in confined spaces,
spoken into existence with their words,
sprung from drops of blood and sweat,
sprouted from tears shed like rain...
children beyond counting,
though the other gods did not know
that such parentage was possible.

Their children were like them,
with similar bodies, similar struggles,
physical forms ranging to more masculine,
fully feminine, and every point between or beyond,
with genitals of many shapes and sizes
and configurations, whether born or built,
created and crafted
or simply cropped and kept.

These children knew pain and exclusion,
rejection and revulsion, misunderstanding,
persecution, pathologization, marginalization,
erasure, hatred, violence, and death
as equally, and greater, and sometimes even lesser
than their parents had known
throughout life and death and life again.

When Panpsyche regarded her brother
and Panhyle gazed at his sister,
both realizing they were no longer
alone in their state nor their struggles
with innumerable offspring on the earth,
suddenly their love for one another
grew, and changed, and transformed.

They had experienced life and death,
their own miraculous births
and the births of their children,
and every vicissitude of existence;
they had the love of parents,
of friends, and of siblings;
but they lacked the love
of lover and beloved.

Panpsyche, a benign siren of a woman,
and Panhyle, a friendly minotaur of a man
suddenly felt an attraction for each other,
a pull not even Zeus could restrain
nor Typhon resist.

And though Zeus may have preferred
to have been the first lover to each,
instead, that pleasure and privilege
the brother and sister, two beings,
would grant one to the other—
as Osiris and Isis, Set and Nephthys,
Ares and Aphrodite, Zeus and Hera.

Hand in hand, they went behind
the cover of closed doors
and remained therein for months.
The earth shook and the sky flamed
with the power and passion
of their unleashed pleasure.

And the very morning after
their love-bout was culminated,
they were accompanied by a new being
as they emerged from their seclusion.

With joy and with great excitement
Hymenaios arrived and blessed their union
and the goddesses of midwifery
came forward to fawn upon the new child.

But, when the divine parents and friends
of Panpsyche and Panhyle demanded
to know who was the father and who the mother,
the contented couple confounded them.

They did not say what had truly happened:
for it was not the love of lovers they shared,
and it was not the union of generation
that had come about between them.

No: their love remained, and increased,
because they knew they were equals,
they respected each other to the utmost
and knew they were complete in themselves.
Nothing the other could add
would make either greater or lesser.

The space between them
hung like an unasked question,
but it was a space that could be filled
by nothing save for the love each bore
for their sibling, pure and unconditional.
They never again questioned the love
that each had for the other,
and that love, filling the space between,
answered back,
and became a being entirely of love.

They knew the truth of the matter,
but were afraid of the thoughts
of all the gathered gods,
their many parents and progenitors.

They were silent and reserved,
and in that place of uncertainty
the others filled it with the fruits
of their expectations,
of what *should* have happened
when love and birth occur.

"I am my daughter's mother,"
Panpsyche announced.

But when she was questioned
whether she had borne the child
from her own body
or carried the child
within her own womb,
Panpsyche silently smiled.

Some derided her for this.

"I am my son's father,"
Panhyle declared.

But when he was questioned
whether he had begotten the child
from his own seed
or had penetrated his spouse
with his own phallus,
Panhyle silently smiled.

And, some also derided him for that.

But what was most confusing to all present,
as equally for Panhyle as for Panpsyche,
was that there was only one being, one child,
who was called "daughter" by one parent
and "son" by the other,
and seemed equally apt
to answer to both.

Though the child resembled both parents
in face and features and body,
and though the child had been born
as fully grown as Athena from Zeus' brow,
the child looked younger and smaller
than either of eir parents.

The effect of this was twofold:
it made all who came into contact with em
want to nurture and protect and love the divine child,
but it also made all and sundry
treat the child—a deathless and immortal deity—
as if e was immature and ignorant, helpless and clueless.

And the child saw this from the first moment.

The gods and ancestors and deified mortals,
the heroes and deceased children of Panhyle and Panpsyche
began arraying themselves in factions
behind the child's two parents.

Those behind Panhyle saw a sturdy son,
skillful at sports and sciences
ready to run or throw a ball
with an enviable penis.
Those behind Panpsyche saw a divine daughter,
devoted and sweet, speaking peaceably,
refined and attentive and sensitive
with budding breasts.

Still, there were a few present
who saw neither of those things
when they looked upon the new child.
Some simply saw a mass of confusion,
conflicting traits assembled together,
an ambiguity of androgynous characteristics.

And though there were elements
to the perceptions of all present
that could be considered correct,
only two who were there
saw the divine child as e truly was:
Antinous and the child emself.

As the gathered crowds shouted and argued
on whether the child's penis or breasts were bigger
and began clambering forward
to clothe the child as each faction preferred,
only Antinous and the child emself
realized that the child was already clothed—
but in that covering, ironically,
the child felt even more naked.

There was a fascination,
an enthrallment, an attraction
that all present felt toward the child,
a curiosity and an intrigue, but also
a desire to possess,
to define, to mold the child
into whatever they wished em to be.

96

The thronging masses in their opposed contingents
pushed onward to engulf the child,
but they were held at bay
when Antinous sprang forward in eir defense.

"No one, be they mother or father,
grandmother or grandfather,
half-sibling or friend or mere bystander,
will touch this child—
my grandest child—
unless e wishes one to do so!"

And one faction heard him say "he"
instead of "e"
while the other heard "she."

The surging mass of divinity
backed away and gave the child space.
E came forward and took Antinous' hand.

"Thank you, grandfather."

Some present there took note
that the first words of the new divine child
were words of gratitude
and honoring of one's ancestors.

"Now," continued Antinous,
"what is your name,
and how would you like to be called?"

The divine child knew the answer,
and began to speak with enthusiasm.

"I am the child of Panpsyche
and the offspring of Panhyle;
I am favored with a noble and extensive lineage;
I am desired of all, and a joy to each;
I am the culmination of all love....
Therefore, it is my wish
to be called by my right name,
which is—"

And though the child did not cough,
it was as if e was choking
and the breath departed
before the word could come out.
E could not speak nor say eir name,
though e knew what it was
in the very fundaments of eir soul
and the deepest marrows of eir body.

And, stranger still to relate,
both of the child's two parents
knew eir name as well,
and when they came forward
to embrace and support their child
and to speak for em,
they could not pronounce the name either,
fumbling on its consonants
and stumbling on its vowels
so that what came from them
was only a mass of confusion.

The child was flustered beyond further speech,
frustrated beyond rational thought,
and simply began to cry.
Eir parents, wishing to comfort their child,
tried to console em and to calm em,
but their efforts were useless.
Antinous, though, stood by em,
embraced em, and wept with em.
Others were moved to do the same.

But, in grief and disappointment,
the surging mass of divinity mostly dispersed,
upset that without a name,
though e was a deathless deity
and a formidable immortal power,
none could call upon em
in spell or in prayer.

X.

$\mathbf{B}$esides the lack of eir own name
the child wanted for nothing,
and was a favor and fortune to all.
The god Pan, container and grandparent,
took especial joy at the child's nature—
the noontime indolence,
the afternoons of play and sport,
the raucousness of the child's dances
and the haunting airs of eir songs.

For lack of a name, the many gods
simply called em "the child,"
and all knew which child was meant.
But, they sexed and gendered the child
how they desired, never asking
how the child emself preferred—
except Antinous, who knew better.

He taught Favorinus, who taught Polydeukion,
who taught Memnon and Achilles,
who taught Regillus, Elpinike and Athenais.
Marguerite Porete understood readily,
and Yeshua likewise knew eir proper address.

100

Hadrian had trouble with it,
as did Herodes and Trajan;
Sabina, Julia Balbilla, Plotina and Matidia,
Marciana and Domitia Paulina
were inconsistent but sincere and concerted in their efforts.

Some of the grandparents of the child
among the gods, heroes, and deified mortals
eventually caught on as well;
but all the while, the child never spoke
and stated what e preferred or desired.

Panpsyche and Panhyle loved their child
as much as they loved all their other children,
but fluctuated between "he" and "she,"
"she" and "he," never saying "e."

And when e would go to bathe
in the pool of the Sangarius River
and would look in the clear mirror
of the water's placid surface,
suddenly a passing breeze
or a distant tremor in the earth
would disturb the water's calmness
and scatter eir image in ripples.

Whether e was clothed or naked
people saw em not as e was,
but how they preferred em.
Even when e had a penis
or eir breasts were displayed,
or when e sported a beard
and eir vulva was visible
the battles of "he" and "she"
in the discourse of the deities
was like enduring a small death,
a gentle but persistent crushing,
a stubbing that felt like a stomping.

But, the child said nothing of this.

One day, the child went with Persephone
to pick flowers in the field,
and they were joined in their leisure
by Artemis, swift in the hunt.
The child would pick a bouquet
and then chase down a hare on foot,
e would make a javelin of fennel
and arrows of rushes
as e ran after deer
on feet more fleet than a Gaulish greyhound.
Flowers and felling, hyacinths and hunting,
jacinth and javelin, the chase and the collection.

The heavens above were sundered in thunder
and the earth below opened in an abyss.
Hades rose up from the fundaments
and Zeus descended from the firmament.
Both seized the arms of the child.

"She is mine, for while Persephone is absent
I will have a lady and mistress in my lands."

"He is mine, for Ganymede needs a playmate
and I another sporting boy for pleasure."

A wave crashed against all parties present
and Poseidon arose from amidst its foam.

"I have been deprived of Nerites from jealousy,
therefore I will have him;
and I have been deprived of Medusa from spite,
therefore I will have her....
though he and she is my own grandchild."

And even Selene, in her chariot above
Veered to the side to gain the child's attention.

The child, with a rage like Typhon
and a might greater than Atlas
at last spoke on eir own behalf.

"None of you will have hide nor hair of me!
I am no one's boy,
I am no one's girl,
I am no one's plaything
and no one's tool!
By my name, beyond knowing,
beyond the powers of sea and sky,
moon and the Styx itself,
depart from me at once!"

As if they were puppets on strings
and the puppeteer departed in haste
with marionettes in hand,
the three gods were drawn back
to their abodes above, below, and beyond,
and the moon overhead resumed her right course.
This was a child not to be trifled with,
nor whose power should be disrespected,
nor whose will should be ignored.

As the years passed, the divine beings
both related and unrelated to the child
convened a council and invited the child
to hear their decrees about em.

Hermes of good speech
delivered the verdict:
"Divine child, the gods among us
and your parents and grandparents
have presented you with an ultimatum:
you must choose between two options
and decide the following dilemma—
either seek another with whom to join in marriage
or pick a sphere of influence over which to preside."

"And why, o speaker of truths
and messenger of the gods,
my own dear grandfather,
have the divine ones judged this necessary?"

"If you cannot define yourself
by your own means and voice,
then you must define yourself
by the choices you make
whether in your way of life
or in your manner of loving."

"That is a despicable condition!"

"Then there is a third option
which the assembled immortals
will impose upon you unwilling:
condemnation to the pit of Tartarus
where your powers will no longer threaten."

And though the child knew e could hold at bay
Poseidon, Hades, and Zeus at once,
e knew that going against all the gods
and dishonoring all eir progenitors
would be both impossible and unwise.

Antinous saw the hurt in eir eyes,
Favorinus shed tears for em,
Set was angry on eir behalf,
and many mothers wept likewise.

"Very well, then—
I will find either a way of love,
or a way of life,
though I know no goddess or god
who would have me as I am,
nor am I acquainted with any deity
that would direct my powers productively."

"You have been given one year
to accomplish this feat—
the day you yourself were born
is one and the same as the birth-feast
of your parents Panpsyche and Panhyle;
therefore, let it be your rebirth
into a renewed life in love
or a newfound vocation—one year hence."

The child sought out many teachers
and yet found none that were suitable.
Though, after several false starts and returns,
e found fellowship and some small success
with Chnoubis and Glykon,
slithering into and out of every sphere,
inhabiting the interstices between worlds,
speaking oracles both true and inflated,
joining deity to deity, form to form,
and shedding skin in renewal frequently.
But, these were not the serpents e sought.

When heavenly planets and far stars were exhausted,
when grain and herb, animal and art,
weather and world, land and light
were all eliminated as options,
an idea occurred to the child.

E sought out the sacred grove
of the Erotes, the collective
where dwelt the gods and goddesses of love.

From a distance, the grove came into view
inhabited by numerous nude figures.

Preeminent among them was Eros eternal,
from before time itself the binding force of the universe.

Anteros, reciprocating love, child of Poseidon and Nerites
stood waiting to return love or vanquish the unrequiting.

Himeros, wild child of Ares and Aphrodite
like an unleashed hound presided over desire.

Pothos, Eros' adopted son born of Iris and Zephyros
stood—like the child—longing at a distance.

Hermaphroditos, the bisexual being,
was there to inspire all loves beyond gender.

Himeros' sister, Harmonia, divine concord, grandmother of Dionysos
created amity and peace between all parties.

Hymenaios was ready to bless each wedding,
and Hedylogos to speak the sweetest flatteries.

The child of Mars and Venus, chubby Cupid
shot flitting arrows of passing fancy and infatuation.

Butterfly-winged Psyche, the soul's deepest desire
reclined with her daughter Hedone, pleasure embodied.

Narcissus and his twin sister Narcissa, newly-born
were the archetypes of self-love, both for good and ill.

The *Numen Homosexualitatis*, lavender-hued,
sent abstracted attractions to all sexes for themselves.

Euphorion, winged child of Achilleus and Helen
was the mortal's desire for ecstatic immortality.

From Egypt's desert sands, golden Hathor of the West—
the child's grandmother—dispensed her blessings, muse of love's arts.

From cold northern lands, Freyr and Freya
gave fertility, love, and fecundity to their devotees.

Swan-winged Óengus and Caer Ibormeith
brought dreams and visions of love to sleepers.

Kama, the enslaving and enlightening desire
was alert to inspire or instill illusions.

Innumerable other beautiful nude winged beings
brought every form of love to mortals from the grove.

It had been so long since the child recalled
eir own name, eir own deepest nature,
and at last, remembering all,
e knew that the grove was eir destiny.
With face beaming, ready to speak at last,
e knew that both love and a way of life
was finally within eir immediate reach.

Wingless, e rushed, slinked, slithered,
shedding layers of sadness and exclusion
as e approached the blessed bright grove.

At the boundary between love's abode
and the world that is so harsh toward love,
the child tripped and faltered.
An invisible barrier held em back.

The Erotes saw the approaching child
and went to embrace em with their many gifts.
But, even with their consent and permission,
the child could still not pass the barrier.

Frustrated, but inspired, the child stripped off
the little remaining clothes e wore,
eager to be unencumbered and nude
like the Erotes who were eir own people,
but the barrier still held em back.

Every one among the Erotes
saw em as e truly was,
called em by words appropriate to eir gender,
and each even came to know eir name,
but none could speak it aloud
until the child spoke it emself.

Even after Aphrodite, wishing the best
for her dearest grandchild
showed em to her sacred spring
to bathe and cleanse emself from all stain...
even after Euphorion and Hathor and Hermaphroditos
tried to help their dearest grandchild however possible...
the barrier, like adamantine armor
would not be penetrated by the divine child.

At last, Eros himself knew the difficulty
and spoke the solution to the problem.

"In the grove of the Erotes,
no hatred can exist.
Though there is love within you,
there is also hate—
not even hate for the other gods
who have imposed this fate upon you,
but the most insidious and destructive hate:
hatred of one's own self.
If you can find a manner
of purging this most difficult demon
from within your own innermost being,
only then will you be able
to enter this grove without impediment.
It will not be easy.
We love you, and will intercede for you.
We will bless you, favor you, and stand by you.
But you must complete this task for yourself."

The insight was like lightning across the black night,
the very presence of divinity amidst darkness.
But, it was also as painful in its reverberations
and as shuddering in its implications.
No lightning, however glorious in its fulminations,
had a weight as great or as immediate as this.

The child, aspiring to the Erotes' realm,
was saddened and disillusioned to realize
that e had hatred within emself.
Narcissus and Narcissa came forward
and made a suggestion.

"Perhaps there is a lack of self-love
within your soul that creates this hate,
or at least allows it a space to thrive.
Find a mirror to see yourself as you truly are,
and, no doubt, you will come to love yourself
as ardently as we have known and loved ourselves."

The Sangarius River, the imperfect mirror,
had failed the child in such attempts before.
But what river would be better?
Not the Nile, nor the Tiber, nor the Orontes,
the Amazon, the Ganges, the Mississippi....

At last, the child knew of one
who was acquainted with hatred,
and who was eir own forgotten grandmother:
Eris, attended by the Erotes' brothers,
Phobos and Deimos.

"Greetings, kinsperson!"

The child was surprised at their recognition.

"You know what I am, then?"

"We see you are one of us,
filled with a deep hatred,
strife, fear...your blood is our own."

"But I do not want to be full of hate!
I do not want to be chained by fear!
I do not wish to be the arena
for the eternal battle with strife!"

Eris laughed. "Then purge yourself."

"I do not know how!"

Deimos and Phobos loomed menacingly,
attempting to intimidate their distant relative.
It did not work.

"Your mettle is stronger than I thought—
but, you are my grandchild, after all.
There is one river that is an infallible mirror
to all that is hateful in gods and mortals:
the River Styx in the realm of Hades,
the river by which you yourself have sworn.
The river's goddess presides indomitable there
in reward for her support of Zeus against the Titans.
Seek your true reflection upon her surface—
though you may not like what you see,
your effort's results will not be disappointing."

The child came to the banks of the Styx
where Charon ferried souls across
and returned with his seats empty,
never leaving a wake on the water's surface.
The black oppressive obsidian darkness
made the water's unfathomable depths
a terrifying reflective surface.

Deimos and Phobos skulked after the child,
hounding eir steps, cajoling from the shadows,
lurking cold and patient and out of sight.

The child, naked and completely honest,
looked at eir own reflection in the Styx,
but what stared back was not emself—
it was herself.
E blinked, and saw what stared back
was not emself, but himself.
E blinked again, and saw not emself,
but a man with a scarred chest and a vulva;
e blinked again, and saw not emself,
but a breasted woman with a penis.
E blinked again, and saw not emself,
but a perfect androgyne;
and e blinked once more, and saw not emself,
but a figure with no gender at all,
no breasts, no body hair, no beard,
no penis, no vulva...
and when e stared at this form longer,
soon it faded and disappeared,
and nothing but a black abyss gaped back.

Phobos and Deimos snickered from the shadows
and quietly heckled and ridiculed the child.

Eir eyes welled up with tears,
having seen that e was as others saw em,
but when e most wanted to be seen for emself
and known and loved for emself
by emself
there was nothing there to see or to love,
but instead only the images e knew e was not,
and all the hate e felt for not being them
and all the hate e felt for not being emself.

Phobos and Deimos now spoke into eir ears,
feeding fear and sadness, desperation and loneliness and self-hate.

It was too much.

The black abyss of the depths of the Styx
yawned wider than the expanse of the cosmos
and seemed the perfect nothingness
into which one might descend,
bereft of all purpose, image, and identity,
to become the absence e felt e was.

"Go ahead—jump. You will not be missed."

The child closed eir eyes
and took a step into the water.
The surface closed over em
without even a ripple.

Phobos and Deimos cackled in self-congratulation
as if they had just defeated an army single-handed.

The Barque of Millions of Years
skimmed across the surface of the Styx
leaving a wide and wavy wake.
Antinous stood at its prow
and with two well-aimed javelin tosses
his liberating darts pierced the flesh
of Phobos in his right arm
and Deimos in his left leg.
The two fled in cowardice.

A hand reached down into the depths
of the Styx to grasp the wrist
of the child who fell into the river.

It was not Thetis, who had bathed Achilleus thus...
It was not Re, the savior of the drowned deified...

It was not even Antinous the Liberator,
who had likewise fallen once
and who had come to assist his grandchild.

112

It was Eris.

When the child emerged fully from the waters
e was transformed, shining,
and not a pore on eir body
was not as strong as a steel-rimmed shield.

As the child's last toe touched the water's surface
before finding refuge in the air above,
the Styx's surface began to froth
like it never had in all the aeons.

A throng of *daimones* emerged from the waves
that had been purged from the child's soul.
There was Androphobia and Gynephobia,
Transphobia, Biphobia, Homophobia, Heterophobia,
Androgynephobia, Panphobia, Autophobia,
and many other *daimones* of fear
that would inspire a soul toward hatred.

But, mixed in with that throng of fearful *daimones*
were another class of spiritual beings:
Androphilia, Gynephilia,
Transphilia, Biphilia, Homophilia, Heterophilia,
Androgynephilia, Panphilia, Autophilia,
and a variety of other angels of affection
that would inspire a soul towards love.

The two throngs would scatter and gather,
would pursue each other,
sometimes winning one over the other,
sometimes losing against their adversaries,
sometimes ignoring each other
and going entirely separate ways.

Antinous tossed his spear to his grandchild;
in the child's outstretched hand, it became a sword.

The waters of the Styx formed a glistening film
on the surface of the child's skin,
reflecting every color under Helios, Selene, and Iris.

With a sheen like silver
and a gleam like gold
the child gazed on eir form
in the dark mirror of the Styx.
There was no phantom idol
of other's expectations
nor the dejected spectre
of eir own defeated ideals
staring back at the child in response;
there was only emself,
exactly as e was,
exactly as e would be,
exactly as e should be,
exactly as e always had been
and ever more shall have been.
E was not male nor female;
e was not female become male;
e was not male become female;
e was not an androgyne;
e was not neuter and sexless.
E was eir own gender
beyond binaries, even if in unity.

E thought of all those other genders,
and all eir parents and grandparents
and the gods and mortals who were each
and e truly loved them all
for being exactly what they were.

And, for the first time
in all eir life,
the child laughed with tears
and an orgasm engulfed eir body
that spread like a seismic shift
to shudder across the cosmos,
bringing a warmly convulsive pleasure
to everything in its wave-front.

The child was happy.

Antinous, who had called the child by eir own pronoun
now knew his grandchild's name
and saw the bodily form that was its fitness.
He invited em on the Barque of Millions of Years
to convey em, not across into Hades,
but back to the grove of the Erotes.

They came on a canal from a river's branch
to the proximity of the grove
and embarked together on foot
for the last expanse of space separating them.

On the verge of the grove
the child feared that the unseen wall
would hold em back as it had before.

"Erotes, kinsfolk, I have come
to be admitted among your ranks."

Eros answered, "In what manner
do you think yourself worthy of entry here?"

"I have purged every kind of hatred
from the depths of my own soul."

"And, by doing thus, you have released
those monstrosities upon the world—
you are a second Pandora!"

"But I have also given birth
to every hatred's antidote,
their cures and their adversaries."

"And yet, there is still within you
a strong spirit of resentment, of rebellion;
you have not exorcised the *daimones*
of anger and rage inside of you.
You come to the abode of every love
bearing an unsheathed sword in your hand."

"But anger runs hot and immediate,
like every madness inspired by the gods—
be it ecstasy, or art, or love itself...
and has our mother Aphrodite herself
not wed in joyous bed Ares
and given birth to Deimos and Phobos,
our kinsmen? And surely Anteros,
the god of reciprocal love
as equally as the avenger of unrequited love
bears pain which becomes anger and resentment
within him on behalf of all spurned lovers,
and yet he is within this grove
and a resident beloved of it!"

"Still, every kind of love that can be imagined
is represented by a deity in this place—
we have no need for others."

"But is there any deity within your grove
who embodies *all* varieties of love?"

"There is not."

"Then allow me to enter the grove:
I am the child of Panpsyche
and the offspring of Panhyle—
I am favored with a noble and extensive lineage;
I am desired of all and a joy to each;
I am the culmination of all love...
I am *Paneros*.
I am the love that conquers everything.
And I will enter this grove
for I already live there."

The sword in eir hand moved without effort
and plunged into the thick of the invisible barrier,
a force that bound the grove of the Erotes
since even before Eros himself had emerged;
like a million pieces of glass, sharpened shards
rained down throughout the cosmos
causing innumerable wounds to its inhabitants
that were as unseen as the barrier itself...
but now, there was no separation
between the dwelling-place of love
and the rest of the universe—
the flowers of every kind of love
could take root anywhere, in everyone
and love would be forever boundless after.

Eros himself had worn unknown chains
made from the same subtle material,
but now it was gone, and he had been freed
even though he had not known he had been bound.

It was the day of eir birth,
and the day of eir parent's birth,
and the decree of the gods had been satisfied:
Paneros had found a place for emself
and had spoken eir own name,
and had found a partner to love—
the entirety of the cosmos,
which, like the unseen boundary of love
was now wedded to Paneros
with a billion times a billion
invisible rings of matrimony,
pledges of undying love and adoration
for the being who made possible
the endless outflowing of love
to the furthest reaches of the universe.

The hum and the thrum
deep within the heart of every being
joined in an ageless harmony
of the spheres and the ages across the cosmos,
a tiny spasm of orgasmic pleasure
that could be kindled to greater heights
and taken to greater depths
whenever love unleashed is recognized.

And Eris was pleased.

XI.

One by one, the many deities and heroes
came to see, to know, and to love Paneros
exactly as e was, in soul and in body.

The other Erotes delighted in their new sibling,
their colleague, their co-conspirator,
and with Paneros' help they put themselves
to their own ranks in the service of spreading love
even more widely and ardently than they had done before.

Paneros was strange, however,
for e had no wings like the others
or like eir mother Panpsyche.
But, this was no limitation
to eir power of flight.
When Paneros brought eir undeniable love
to any god, mortal, or hero
it was not suspended in the air above
and prone to flit away like bird or butterfly;
it was a love that settled and rested,
that coiled around its object, constricting,
making its object shed its skins
like a serpent in renewal.

There was no potential lover so cold
or so secluded behind stone walls
that Paneros could not find a crack
which would become a by-way
for eir slithering insinuation,
the entry and infestation of eir love.

In the legions of love, with diligence,
Paneros rapidly went from raw new recruit
to honored and decorated field commander;
even Eros himself praised Paneros
to his mother Aphrodite, to his wife Psyche,
and to all the gods above and below himself.

Paneros' mother and father, Panpsyche and Panhyle,
were pleased to have a child like Paneros,
so clearly born of eir parents
and yet so distinct and different.

But, like eir parents,
Paneros felt alone,
for there was no other like em in the cosmos.
Though e was able to love emself,
to love others, and to be loved in return,
there was no equal and partner to eir love,
no colleague and companion to eir being.
Aphrodite had Ares, Eros had Psyche,
and even Panhyle had Panpsyche
(though each had other lovers innumerable),
but Paneros had no lover of eir own alone.

Paneros' children, however, slowly multiplied,
often silent, misunderstood and secluded
in the world of mortals;
like a thousand mirrors, the drops of water
from the Styx that had clung to eir body
as if they were a thousand lovers on fire,
each drop fell into the soul of a mortal
that soon found e was like Paneros—
another gender entirely,
or able to love all equally.

The pleasures of the children
like a deep blue wave of warm pressure
flowed and fired through the perineum
of the divine parent Paneros,
sending ripples of healing golden bliss
to every limb of eir body.

And every hatred and offense
and failure of understanding,
every lack of recognition
and word of derision
turned Paneros' flashing blade
around at eir own heart;
a thousand times it plunged in,
a thousand times e wailed in anguish,
a thousand times it was pulled out,
a thousand times a thousand drops of blood fell,
and a thousand times the wound closed
and the sword was sharpened,
burnished brightly and finely honed
from the blood and pain of Paneros.

The blood within em, it seemed,
wanted to escape, to have its own outlet,
to become something Paneros was not
and never would nor wanted to be.

But, simply falling on the ground
did not yield fruit nor flowers
to the desire of Paneros' blood.

Glykon and Chnoubis, Ananke and Ophioneus,
and every serpent of the heavens and the earth
and every dragon imprisoned in Tartarus
did not have any advice for Paneros—
except for one.

Climbing higher and higher into the ether,
slinking and slithering ever-upward
in a manner only spiritual snakes know how to do,
Paneros eventually reached the domain
of Damballah and his seven thousand coils.
Ayida Weddo and Erzulie Freda, his wives, were there.
Unlike Quetzlcouatl, serpent and rainbow in one,
and also unlike emself,
the white cascades of Damballah's endless form
were wedded to the body of his wife,
Ayida Weddo, the beauteous spectrum.
Like the ineffable voice of eir grandmother, Hekate,
Paneros listened to the speaking serpent
in the tongues of divine celestial fire.

E knew what e had to do.

Paneros went to eir mother and eir father
and spoke the necessary words,
the whisper of pulsing plasma
and the speech of celestial flame.
It was the same speech spoken
by Zeus to Persephone to birth Zagreus,
by Zeus to Semele when she was smitten to ash,
and by Sabazios to Bendis when Kotys was born.

The parents and child secluded themselves
in a cave, sealed themselves in with a stone.

The desire in Paneros' blood to come forth
soon was given shape, container, form
in another being, the child of the child,
the child of the parents,
the three that together made one—
another one.

Though e still sometimes turned the sword around
and even felt its point penetrate eir heart,
Paneros never again bled in anguish
once eir new child was born.

XII.

Whelp the three parents had done their work
in conceiving the child and bringing it to birth
they returned again into the light
from the depths of the dark cavern
and left its mouth open
for whatever might come in the future.

The child resembled its mother Panpsyche,
its father Panhyle, and its progenitor Paneros.
And yet, it was different than all
for it combined every feature of each
but still had more features unique only to it.

Great hope and excitement
accompanied the three parents.

Panpsyche spoke first:
"This new child
will be the agent
and the culmination
of every wish for peace
among gods and mortals;
she will be called
Paneirene."

124

Panhyle spoke next:
"This new child
will be a speaker
and the advocate
of every kind of truth
among gods and mortals;
let him be called
Panaletheia."

Paneros spoke third:
"This new child
is already the bearer
and the exemplar
of every type of beauty
among gods and mortals;
may e be called
Pankalos."

But the child hirself
had the last word.
"Let there be peace
among my three parents.
Let there be total truth
in their words and mine.
Let only brightest beauty
be seen by them in me.
And let my own power
show forth in my actions.
I am Paneirene by Panpsyche,
I am Panaletheia by Panhyle,
I am Pankalos by Paneros;
but by myself, by my own power,
I am *Pancrates*."

The name like the sundering of Chaos
and the echo of forgotten singularities
spread like the pull of gravity
across the universe's panorama.
Pancrates was born.

Unlike Panpsyche and Panhyle
and any deity before,
Pancrates was not one gender
no matter what body sie was in.
Unlike Paneros, unique in the world,
Pancrates was not another gender
that may not have been recognized.
Pancrates, like hirself,
like hir increasing children on earth,
was every gender, including none.
The atmosphere around hir
burned because of the manner
every energy manifested in hir
without separation nor loss to entropy.

Pancrates enjoyed piloting the chariot
of Cú Chulainn, one of hir grandparents.
Too young, too bold, too beautiful,
Cú Chulainn knew the power of Pancrates,
a power that when unleashed could destroy worlds,
or alter them in inconceivable ways.
It would take more than three cauldrons
to calm the ardor of Pancrates if it was raised.

Cú Chulainn, too, knew the pain
that could result from gender misunderstood,
from a body that is unusual;
envious eyes easily become resentful,
lovers and brothers and friends could be lost.

Achilleus as well, with Helen at his side
and Patroklos playing the charioteer
empathized with his colleague Cú Chulainn
and with the plight of Pancrates.

"My mother, Thetis, was forbidden
from having offspring with Poseidon or Zeus
for fear the resulting child
would overthrow the Olympian lineage."

126

Antinous interjected, "And yet, Pancrates,
both Achilleus the offspring,
and Thetis, and Poseidon
are among the parents of your progenitors..."

"It is no wonder, then," Polydeukion joined in,
"that Zeus was so insistent on possessing,
or destroying, Panpsyche and Panhyle from birth."

"Likewise," Achilleus mused further,
"that he destroyed Euphorion, my son..."

"But, as all know," Polydeukion continued,
"who have passed through the holy fires of Eleusis—
as Demophoön was passed by Demeter—
that the potential of divinity is within all,
divinity that even the gods
must reckon with as equals.
You, Pancrates, were born from that fire."

"Titanic overthrow," Antinous replied,
"need not be the only result of such things.
The gods, for all of their power and majesty,
are profoundly insecure, and considering
the manners via which they came to power,
it is no wonder that such fear reigns supreme
even among the mightiest of Olympians.
Herakles, Asklepios, the Dioskouroi, and Dionysos
have known the scorn of the gods for mingling
mortal presence with divine power.
By even upsetting the tenuous, fragile balance
between male and female, that stasis
set since after Chaos reigned,
as some of these hero-gods did before you,
the entire system threatens to collapse.
It is no wonder that they fear you!
I do not fear that you, Pancrates,
will overthrow the gods, but
I fear what they will fear of you."

If some of the gods feared Paneros' power,
Pancrates' own potency was infinitely greater—
within hir footsteps, it seemed,
new universes, new aeons
threatened to erupt at the slightest nudge,
negating the present cosmic realm...
Time, space, eternity itself
seemed in danger by Pancrates' very existence.

Many of the gods spoke with Antinous,
who spoke with his children, Panhyle and Panpsyche,
who spoke with their child, Paneros,
who spoke with eir sibling and offspring, Pancrates.
The worries of all were expressed openly.

"If the stability of the cosmos
is undermined by my existence,
then I will prove to everyone
that I am its buttress,
its pillar, and its keystone
rather than its downfall."

Panpsyche, Panhyle, and Paneros
accompanied their child, Pancrates
in the Barque of Millions of Years
with Antinous the Navigator at the helm.
The parents and grandparents of these gods
joined in their journey
to the edges of reality.

After an hour, or an age,
they came to the first
of three beings: Aion,
wreathed with a serpent,
bearing breasts and a penis,
holding a key, standing on an orb,
lion-headed and lightning-voiced.

"Divine Aion, guardian and embodiment
of this age, of previous ages, and every age to come,
greeting!"

But none among the many gods, heroes, or divine mortals
needed to say another word to celestial Aion,
spanning the height of the universe.
The eyes of Aion like winged, haloed stars
blazing like galaxies in spinning space
saw the child, Pancrates,
and was pleased.
The key in Aion's hand
became a double-headed axe,
and with one swing of it,
Aion removed Aion's own head,
and the body fell to its knees.
The head descended, diminishing,
until it was the size of any lion's head.
Pancrates caught the head in its descent.
Sie wore it like a crown, like a cloak's cowl,
and sie was like a maned lioness ever after.
Aion was as before, unmoved—
the passing of one age into another
was nothing new for divine Aion.

After an age, or an hour,
they came to the second
of three beings: Abraxas,
combed cock-headed,
breastplate-encased,
with serpents for legs
holding a whip and a shield.

"Divine Abraxas, guardian and embodiment
of time and space, matter and energy,
movement and stillness, stasis and transformation,
greeting!"

But none of the many gods, heroes, or divine mortals
needed to say another word to supernal Abraxas,
branching the breadth of the universe.
The ears of Abraxas, like black holes
brimming with every bit of information within them
heard the name of Pancrates
and was pleased.
Though they had seen the body,
none of the divine beings present saw
that Abraxas was within its own chariot;
it relinquished the reins of the vehicle
and, diminished, turned it over to another.
The whip of guidance, the shield of defense
it likewise passed to a new recipient.
Pancrates took up the reins of the chariot.
Sie wore the shield on her back
and grasped the whip, holding it in reserve.
Abraxas, as before, was unchanged—
loss and gain, transmission and motion
was ever the way with Divine Abraxas.

After an age, and after an hour,
after an instant, and after an eternity,
and before they had set out
and even before the first of them was born,
they came to the last
(who was the first)
of the three beings: Phanes,
the pure and unencumbered light
of beauty, knowledge, truth,
being, divinity, and essence
in all the universe
surrounded by galactic clusters
and embroidered with a panoply
of multiversal vignettes—
eagle-winged, bull-horned, serpent-draped, lion-maned,
and the very image in gender
of Pancrates hirself.

130

"Hail and praise to you, O Light of Lights,
O Flower of Flowers, O Star of Stars,
O Divine of Divinities, O God of Gods—
source and serenity, end and essence,
firstborn of beings, illuminator of truths,
greetings, hail, and all praises to you,
Phanes Cosmocrator!"

But nothing needed to happen
after such a hailing.
The many gods, heroes, and divine mortals
found themselves where they had started,
watching themselves have the conversation
that resulted in trial, in council,
in birth of Panhyle and Panpsyche—
but the two divine beings
and their child Paneros
and Pancrates hirself stood among them
watching this scene,
and the scene of every divine and mortal birth
and life and death, love and suffering
of each of them back to their earliest origins.
And when they all looked in wonder
from this scene's unfolding into the past,
the obvious conclusion as to its future
was a question immediately answered
when they turned their attentions toward Pancartes,
who was hirself the image of Phanes,
the wielder of Abraxas' sovereignty,
the embodiment of Aion's majesty.
Time, space, and eternity were all in Pancrates.
There was no power greater among the gods.

The universe's continuous and complete unfolding
could be reversed and undone easily
by the all-powerful Pancrates.

And every one among the gods was afraid.

But their fears were entirely misplaced.
Pancrates, who was called Paneirene,
had no malice toward anyone, god nor mortal,
and no wish for destruction.
Pancrates, who was called Panaletheia,
knew every injustice and violence
that was occurring to hir children.
Pancrates, who was called Pankalos,
also felt deep within hir marrows and sinews
every pleasure and triumph of hir children,
and her many siblings upon the earth
who were the daughters of hir mother Panpsyche,
the sons of hir father Panhyle,
and the offspring of hir blood-giver Paneros.
In soul, in body, in love, she was united to all...

However, there was work to be done.

Though strife is not unavoidable with existence,
for both Eris and Set were hir ancestors,
Pancrates knew that threats to peace
still existed in the world above, below, and beyond.
Hatred and chaos tore at the fabric of justice
and words of dissent and discrimination
rang painfully and sounded discordant
in the ears of the many gods.

With sun-jumping, mace-wielding Hanuman,
with torch-bearing, formless-fired Hekate,
with lion-slaying, Cerberus-taming Herakles,
and with Antinous leading a retinue of heroes,
Pancrates ranged across the worlds
Pursuing every daimon of hatred and discrimination.

Like a herd of cannibalistic cattle,
like a flock of sacrilegious sheep,
they were driven to a precipice.

Alongside Cú Chulainn's barbed chariot,
in which the warp-spasm broke through him,
Pancrates became the smoldering iron,
the firebrand of battle and the burning of purgation
as sie drove the *daimones* off the cliff.

Cautes raised his torch,
and Cautopates lowered his likewise,
and Mithras, god of the median,
slayed the bull as ever he had before,
but the pack of mongrel curs,
the crowd of raging *daimones*
was not slain by spear nor sword
of Pancrates or any other being.

To the last, the horde of savage *daimones*
was swallowed up by Apophis,
the devouring serpent of destruction—
but they did not die, they were not annihilated,
instead they only strengthened
the venomous constrictor of the cosmos.

Upon the celestial Barque of Re
the red god Set arrived,
ready as ever, prepared, as always
to strike the snake-slaying spear upon Apep.
But Set's grandchild, Pancrates,
would not let hir grandfather face it alone.

Seeing his grandchild,
offspring of his own flesh's flesh,
heir of his own molten blood,
Set smiled with a grin
both devious and full of pride.
If Pancrates failed in hir attempt
to slay the Apophis menace,
then he would do as he'd always done.

When they approached the astral anaconda
with its dazzling diamond eyes glinting,
Pancrates plunged off the solar ship
and pursued the serpent by chariot.
Though its length was nowhere near
the seven-thousand coils of Damballah,
it seemed nearly as large, and fifty times as fierce.

The snake spotted the chasing chariot
and struck swift and cobra-quick
to snatch Pancrates in its devouring jaws
and swallowed hir whole, chariot and all.

But a serpent's esophagus,
no matter how swelled with bile,
is much like any other road—
sometimes swerving right, sometimes left.

The residences of the *daimones*
that were swallowed earlier
already sprawled like spoiled suburbs
along the highway of Apophis' innards.

Refineries belching billows
of sulfurous squalid smoke
produced endless barrels of crudeness:
persecution became policy,
hatred became holy writ.

Every kind of love, every expression of gender
was locked away in prison-houses
shielded from light, deprived of breath,
starving and tortured and terrified.

The pollution and conspicuous consumption
of this army of *daimones*
was at home inside Apophis,
but no less appalling for it.

Pancrates knew sie could take the fight
to the streets, to the houses,
to a policy of scorched earth
and total war inside the serpent,
but a melee of one *daimon* at a time
to death or defeat would take an age—
and though Pancrates had ages upon ages to spare,
there were more enjoyable tasks
to be tackled once victory was assured,
and time continued to press onward
for the children in this world who were thus oppressed.

Pancrates drove the chariot onward,
yoked with two serpent steeds:
Glykon on the right,
Chnoubis on the left.
With celerity like a meteor's streak
and an expanse like a comet's passage,
Pancrates spurred the serpents onward
until the ends of Apophis were in sight.

The cavernous creature's space decreased
until it came to a point
inside the tip of its tail.

Without needing to apply the whip
the two hirsute snakes
knew the plans of Pancrates,
whose power over all things
even extended to the Apep serpent's flesh.

It was as if time and time, age and age
passed in an instant, a moment,
and Apophis' skin shed and shed and shed,
sloughing off layer after layer
becoming more than it was to begin with,
evolving into something entirely new.

What was reptilian became avian;
what had been reptilian became aquatic;
what would have been reptilian became mammalian;
and what resulted was neither fish, fowl, or ophidian—
the flesh, the bones, the blood, the sinews, the skin
of Apophis, after endless layers of shedding
became an image, beautiful and animate,
of Pancrates hirself in hir chariot.

Like a pilot within, a puppeteer inside,
Pancrates directed the image of Pancrates
to move about swiftly, dragging the hind end
of Apophis' nether regions about with it
as if it were a different being altogether.

The blackened scales under piles of sloughed skin
on the back end of the devouring serpent,
lost in the depths of the dark cosmos
were like a disguise and a deception—
the serpent Apophis, not knowing itself,
did not ever see, nor even look for,
its own tail, nor would have recognized it
even if it did not appear as Pancrates.

Chaos unbridled ensures its own demise.

Seeing the enemy it had so soon devoured, despised,
emerging from deepest space unscathed,
Apophis attacked again, advancing
like forking electricity across the sky,
clamping down on the image of Pancrates
while Pancrates hirself was freed
from a wound inflicted by the serpent's own fangs.

The enraged serpent, chomping and swallowing
was maddened by the sting of its own poison
bringing about its self-destruction
rather than its usual regeneration
as it devoured itself both within and without.

The cities of the *daimones*
were desolated, and their prisons
were thrown open, the captives escaping
through fissures they themselves fashioned
in the bloated snake's flesh.

The cosmos-spanning serpent
reduced itself to an *ouroboros*,
a lemniscate ring around nothingness,
shrinking significantly in size.

Glykon threaded through one loop
and Chnoubis through the other
and brought its spinning stasis
down to Set on the Barque of Re.
Still smiling, he carefully threaded it
around the shaft of his spear
where it would be safe and stable.

Though some would have said, therefore,
that Set's task was over, for Apophis
no more would threaten Re's nightly passage,
it was not true—for Apophis yet lived,
however it could do no harm
and Set's spear was indeed through its flesh
from one end to the other;
and each day, with Set ever-vigilant,
ready to squeeze the snake with his fist
if it came uncoiled and raged abroad,
the sun came forth whole from the *Amduat*.

And it was by Pancrates' power,
by Paneros' love,
by Panhyle's body and Panpsyche's soul
that all of this was possible.

An Allegory
of Emanations

Oftentimes spiritual experiences of all sorts come in a kind of "spiritual download" format, and even after one thinks one has "unzipped" the file in question, more can seem to spring up on it rather unexpectedly.

I asked myself the question in late November and early December of 2011: why do the births of the Tetrad—Panpsyche, Panhyle, Paneros, and Pancrates—come in the order that they do? Why do the two most gender-flexible figures in this new myth come last, when, strictly speaking, in non-human nature (and often in traditional cosmologies) they came first? I didn't pray this or ask it aloud in any manner, but I got a very full-fledged answer on it almost instantly...And, while it may not be an answer that is appealing to everyone, it is an answer that makes a lot of sense to me.

In many modern pagan formulations, "body" always comes before "soul/spirit/mind," or anything else. Body-primacy is a truly wonderful and useful concept, and has been a great antidote to so much of the spiritual tendency of the Western (and Eastern) world to place the most emphasis and focus upon "matters of the spirit"—indeed, even the term "spirituality" seems to put an emphasis in a particular non-material direction rather than a material one. I do think that the trend toward body-primacy is an important and useful

138

trend overall, and it can be very liberating and wonderful to engage in things like this...or, as someone I know once paradoxically phrased the matter, "ecstatic embodiment."

And yet, there are situations in which body-primacy becomes very problematic. Disability is one of them: what does one do with those bodies that don't "work right," and that left to their natural processes would cause death for those who have them?[15] Transsexuality and transgender status is another such situation. Yes, certainly, there are some trans people who are completely secure and integrated in their gender identity even in their "default" bodily configuration,[16] but I know very few of them, and they are often the ones that are most subjected to misunderstanding and mistreatment in my experience, even in the most casual of situations.

A kind of gender essentialism can often come into body-primacy, and rather unexpectedly at that; a person's gender identity can be written off with statements like "Well, we're all combinations of masculine and feminine energies, and we need to get in touch with both," which often means "I don't understand you and don't want to even attempt to do so," and often with an implied "you big tranny freak" thrown into the mix as well. And, the more patronizing the tone on this matter, the more likely the latter is implied, I think—at least in my own experience.

So, instead of having the experience of getting in touch with one's body, and that process leading to one getting in better touch with one's soul, trans people often have the opposite results: the body is found wanting, and the only real way to go forward is to get in touch with one's soul and one's deepest nature, no matter what one's body might happen to be "saying" by its genital configuration and other physical characteristics. For trans people, as well as gender-variant people more widely, I think the soul comes before the body, as it were.

Thus, it makes sense that Panpsyche is the first of the Tetrad to come into

---

[15] If your answer is anything but "give them the care and assistance that they need," you can stop reading this now and go do something else for a very long time...

[16] If I understand correctly, some such individuals refer to themselves as "transgender but cissexual."

existence. Panhyle follows closely behind, of course (in more ways than one!), but Panpsyche is the first one. The birth of these first two beings is brought about by a huge number of divine figures, of many different genders, including many of the deities who have been called trans in some fashion from many cultures, but aren't "trans-as-such" because the cultures concerned didn't have that particular understanding of gender in the premodern periods. Even various two-spirit peoples in Native American cultures aren't "trans" exactly either, because their gender *is what it is* and it simply is a matter of the rest of the society and the individual recognizing that it isn't among the choices in the typical binary.

And, very interestingly to me, Panpsyche is very definitely male-to-female. While there were a number of female-to-male trans people in early 20th century history, including Michael Dillon, the first sex reassignment procedures performed were done by Magnus Hirschfeld, and involved transitions from male to female. The first widely known trans person in twentieth century history was Christine Jorgensen.[17]

But, we see a kind of pattern developing here: male-to-female transsexuality has been more prominent in the wider culture, and was an earlier "surgical" phenomenon, than female-to-male. I remember as a kid, I saw images of trans women on television (often on "shocker" news journal programs, talk shows, and the like) on a semi-regular basis, but wasn't even aware of the phenomenon of trans men until later in life. Now, of course, I am friends and regular associates with many more trans men than trans women...which is interesting, at least to me!

In many respects, I think we can read something into this developing picture about wider society as well: while it is "understandable" that women might want to become men in a patriarchal and male-dominated society, the idea of a male giving up male privilege, and having parts of one's anatomy removed or altered that carry such a huge amount of symbolic weight and through which the entire axis of male identity is run, is to be profoundly counter-cultural, and therefore both challenging and even threatening to a society that is entirely built on that

---

[17] All three–Dillon, Hirschfeld, and Jorgensen–are *Sancti* of the Ekklesía Antínoou, I might add. And, Dillon and Jorgensen were born in the month of May. Indeed, I wonder if certain zodiac signs are more prone to have trans natives.

model of gender dominance. I'm not saying it's "right," and I certainly don't agree with it, but I think it is fair to say that this is the case.

So, Panpsyche comes first, and she's definitely a (trans) woman, but then Panhyle (who is definitely a [trans] man) follows soon after. The entire matter of "matter" and materiality of the body comes after the birth of the soul, in this case. And, by coming after, it actually has the effect of affirming body-primacy, in a strange way, by asserting that materiality (which is what *hyle* means, after all!) *is important* and needs to be taken seriously, honored, and valued, whether that bodily materiality is redefined spiritually or physically. I don't know many trans people who have not had some intervention to change their outward appearance, whether it is simply a change of wardrobe or hairstyle, going on hormones, or having sex reassignment surgery—all have done something to bring their outer reality more into accord with their inner reality, and each will make whatever choice in that regard is most appropriate for them. So, while I often render Panhyle as "All-Body," the fact that *hyle* means "matter" more generally and widely, I think, acknowledges this dimension that bodily affirmation and integrity is not always a matter (as it were!) of the physical body itself, but instead of some other physical characteristics (like clothes) that are associated with it. There is a level of meaning here in which Panhyle is not only female-to-male, but also has relevance for the larger developmental process involved with many trans and gender-variant people.

And, Paneros follows next, and then eventually Pancrates comes from all the combined efforts of the previous three. Paneros is not actively gendered at all, or is very actively non-gendered, depending on how one might wish to view em; as I am metagendered, I think of Paneros as primarily metagendered.[18] I've sometimes said that to be metagendered is not to be transgendered, but it is also not to be cisgendered; however, as I reflect on this more, I think it is also that both terms are equally true and accurate. Just as a trans woman is a woman from birth gender-wise, but with a body that does not match her gender, I too feel that

---

[18] For some interpretations of metagender, see Phillip A. Bernhardt-House, "So, Which One is the Opposite Sex?: The Sometimes Spiritual Journey of a Metagender," in Tracie O'Keefe and Katrina Fox (eds.), *Finding the Real Me: True Tales of Sex and Gender Diversity* (San Francisco: Jossey-Bass, 2003), pp. 76-87; and the short statement in Robyn Ochs and Sarah E. Rowley (eds.), *Getting Bi: Voices of Bisexuals Around the World* (Boston: Bisexual Resource Center, 2009), p. 101.

I have been the gender I am from birth (and I recall these feelings as far back as age 3), but it has not been one that society recognizes, or for which there is a particular or distinct body or genital configuration. Thus, I am cisgendered from my own viewpoint, even though I'm transgendered from the viewpoint of society.

As a side matter, I'd note that in the post-PantheaCon 2012 discussions, many cisgendered women (whether or not they are affirming of the womanhood of trans women) have resisted the terminology of "cisgender," feeling it is an unfair imposition, and something that trans women (and trans men!) have forced upon them. Though cisgender is not in any way pejorative, unfortunately, I can see some validity in this viewpoint and this resentment on the part of some women. The term "cisgender" does, in essence, assume that society's labeling of a person's gender was "right" from birth, and very few people like to be told that any aspect of their identity is expectable, typical, or even societally-sanctioned. It sort of muddles the issue further that trans people have known that from birth they have been a different gender, and the notion therefore that they have "changed" their gender is entirely incorrect, they've only corrected the labeling that society has put upon them. Cisgender is certainly much preferable to the terms "woman-born-woman" or "genetic women," for example, that have been used to exclude trans women, and it simply seeks to give an accurate labeling of individuals that acknowledges the reality of gender diversity and the possibility that there are women and men who can be trans- or cis-, but it is also not an ideal term by any stretch of the imagination.

I've long had a great deal of discomfort with the entire notion of "gender dysphoria" as it applies to gender variance widely, as well as to trans people in particular. It isn't that there is any "dysphoria" in the trans individual in terms of their own gender identity, it's that there is a stigma attached to having a gender that doesn't fit society's expectations when one has particular external sex (and particular genital) characteristics or configurations. The problem is not from within so much as it is one imposed from without, therefore. I hope that perhaps we can move to a position someday in which anyone and everyone is viewed as potentially transgender in the sense that everyone is potentially "transgressively gendered," and may have characteristics that do not fit the expectable or typical gender norms, no matter what their gender may be. But, that is a long way off at present...and, a much larger issue than can be dealt with reasonably here.

I think the emergence of Paneros as third in the line of the Tetrad follows the development of modern gender-variant consciousness: some might want to change their gender (and they're probably in the majority amongst those who are gender-variant), but some don't want any part of the gender system as it currently exists, up to and including any conception of androgyny or notions of combinatory gender like it. The concept of metagender, I think, is in this category as well. But, such formulations of gender, I don't think, would have been possible without the work of all the trans people who came before, in every respect.

Historically, thus, Paneros must come after Panpsyche and Panhyle; but, further, on a mythic and symbolic level, "love" can only come after the "soul" has come into being, and the "body" has also been fully grasped and accepted (whether in a changed or altered form, or simply as it was at birth).

Finally, we get a deity who is pangendered, and who can have any (and all) of the characteristics of the deities who came before. And, this is a uniquely powerful being; but, unlike the beings that often stand at the "beginning" of many myths of cosmology and cosmogenesis, Pancrates is not a being in which differentiated genders are mere latent potentials, they're all fully expressed, and thus Pancrates stands at the entirely opposite end of the "creation spectrum" or "continuum," one might say. Where all potential existed at the beginning in the first being, all realization and all manifestation exists at the end.

Therefore, in the TransMythology conception of the Tetrad, soul comes first, followed closely by body, from which comes love, and which leads to power: Panpsyche, Panhyle, Paneros, Pancrates.

This entire excursus had relevance and correlations to both history, "trans developmental psychology" (in however pedestrian a way...?!?), and ultimately, by its expression thus, it makes of the TransMythology project not only a mythological construction, but a theological one.

Further Emanations

Since the time when I first introduced the Tetrad to the wider world in late November of 2011, a variety of further occurrences have built the Tetrad's cultus and their reality for me and for a number of other people. In addition to producing the sigil for the Tetrad on the back cover of the present book, Michael Sebastian Lvx has also created a ceremonial-magic-, Thelema-, and Gnosticism-based ritual for the Tetrad, which can be found on his blog.[19] I hope to perform it on many occasions in-person with whomever would like to participate in it, and I'm certain that some form of it will occur each year on the feasts of the Tetrad in March, as well as at other times as desired or needed.

At PantheaCon 2012 in February, I introduced the Tetrad to the group who gathered for the Circle of Cerridwen's "Open Discussion of Gender and Transgender in Paganism" on Sunday the 19th. In the ritual, Sarah Thompson was embodying the energies of Lilith, Jesus, and the Buddha; one of the warders for a direction was carrying Set; Hekate was also invoked at the beginning of the ritual; and one of the other discussion attendees brought Loki's presence to the proceedings. All of these named figures[20] are among the parents of Panpsyche and Panhyle. I was carrying the Tetrad quite strongly during the discussion, and not only speaking their names aloud, but being in the presence of so many of their children, and having several of their divine parents so clearly embodied in the room, was quite an emotional experience for me.

On Monday the 20th, in my session presented under the auspices of the Ekklesía Antínoou, entitled "Super-Syncretism!: Creating Connection while Preserving Diversity," I elaborated a bit further on the syncretistic elements that went into the creation of their myth. Afterwards, in the discussion that followed, Sarah Thompson was present, and said that in many respects, the divine energies she

---

[19]   http://michaelseblux.wordpress.com/2012/03/03/synaxis-of-the-antinoopolian-tedrad/ and http://michaelseblux.wordpress.com/2012/03/04/mystery-feast-of-the-tetrad-of-antinoopolis/

[20] While I would normally not do this, I am here taking "the Buddha" as being a bit more widespread and monistic than I would usually, thus to potentially include Kuan Yin, Kannon, and Avolakiteshvara, who appear in the myth above. If nothing else, those three are definite carriers of "Buddha-nature" and as bodhisattvas are emissaries of superlative compassion.

144

was carrying in the discussion the day before included what could be considered figures who are "all-soul, all-body, all-love, and all-power." While I had certainly met and spoken very briefly with Sarah at the previous PantheaCon, she had not been given any details on the work I was doing, and had not read (to my knowledge) any of the blog entries I had produced on these subjects in the previous three months.

And, in the aftermath of PantheaCon 2012, on March 8th (which is International Women's Day), the Amazon Priestess Tribe of Come As You Are Coven—the group whose Lilith ritual at PantheaCon 2011 was an apparent cause of so much controversy—announced that they were "retiring" from the Z. Budapest[21] lineage of Dianic witchcraft, were changing their name to the Bloodroot Honey Priestess Tribe within CAYA Coven, and they announced the foundation of the Pan-Dianic lineage of witchcraft. Indeed, the Tetrad's presence is felt and recognized in the very name of this new, trans-inclusive lineage of the Dianic tradition!

For cultic practice, honoring the Tetrad on particular dates may be of especial effectiveness. The birthdate of Panpsyche, Panhyle, and Paneros is March 2nd, while the birthdate of Pancrates is March 17th. International Transgender Day of Remembrance, which is on November 20th, is also an important day to honor them, and to involve the Tetrad in remembrance of their honored children slain by violence, as well as the date on which the Tetrad became known to a wider public.

Using the elemental, directional, and animal associations of the various members of the Tetrad is also something that lends itself easily to adaptation to whatever magical or devotional system you use.

A shorthand text that has also proven useful in bringing the Tetrad's presence to a ritual is the "Carol of the Tetrad," which is given subsequently in the present

---

[21] The remarks of Z. Budapest after PantheaCon 2011 were some of the most offensive and hateful remarks in the entirety of this discussion, and though she apologized for having caused hurt feelings before her ritual at PantheaCon 2012, she still used offensive language in excluding trans women from her ritual, and had some disparaging off-the-cuff remarks about trans people being "colorful" and having "interesting outfits," thus refusing to acknowledge the reality of their gender identities.

volume: it also has the advantage of being to a tune (the Christmas carol "We Three Kings") that is familiar to most people! In absence of a full recitation of *All-Soul, All-Body, All-Love, All-Power*, this shorter text can be used as a ready-made invocation until further such texts are developed, or until you are able to write your own.

Π • Π • Π • Π

About six months after the release of the present volume, I will issue a call for submissions, and will begin the work of compiling a follow-up volume to this one, in which I hope that the Tetrad will have taken root in other people's practices. This follow-up volume will contain essays, personal accounts, and poetry and prose detailing expansions of the Tetrad's myths, as well as views of the Tetrad from the perspectives of the many deities—whether their divine and deified mortal parents, allies or antagonists as detailed in the myth above, or of figures not mentioned therein who have come into the Tetrad's orbit in individual and communal practices—as reflected in the writings of those deities' devotees. I hope that this collaborative project of developing cultus to these figures is facilitated by these sorts of actions, whether they are organized by myself or not.

It seems that the Tetrad are coming into the world quite strongly, in the experiences of many people, and I am pleased to be a part of this process, and will be an eager witness to how this process further unfolds. This divine emergence and evolution will no doubt continue with rituals and events at PantheaCon 2013, and on other occasions as well, including the further iterations of the Tetrad's myths and other appearances of them in many media.

May those who love, bless, and praise the Tetrad, and the many gods connected to them, be loved by, blessed by, and praised by the Tetrad and by the many gods in turn!

Carol
of the Tetrad

[sung to the tune of "We Three Kings"]

We Four Beings, of six-pointed star—
cleansing waters; fires that char;
earth, enduring;
air, ensuring
voice for those near and far.

CHORUS: *Oh, Star of Wonder, Star of Light,*
Star of Splendrous Truth and Right;
Westward streaming
Justice beaming-
bring us hope and love tonight!

Firstborn being, Panpsyche am I
soaring like an eagle through sky;
Sister, mother
like no other
over the earth I fly.

CHORUS

148

Second being, I'm Panhyle,
Brother, twin to Panpsyche;
Man with bull's horns
sire of male-borns
in spite of flesh's display.

CHORUS

Paneros, the serpent of love
raining down from heaven above;
Lover's mystery
shall make history
seeing what I'm made of.

CHORUS

Pancrates, completion and close,
Genders' strain I fight and oppose;
Lion, raging
now presaging
freedom which sweetly flows.

CHORUS

Set, Vitalis, fathers two,
from our birth they've seen us through;
Haec est unde
Vita Venit!
Life and love is for you!

CHORUS x 2

About the Author

P. Sufenas Virius Lupus is metagender, and is the founder of the Ekklesía Antínoou—a queer, Graeco-Roman-Egyptian syncretist reconstructionist polytheist group dedicated to Antinous, the deified lover of the Roman Emperor Hadrian and related divine figures—as well as a contributing member of the Neos Alexandria group, and a practicing Celtic Reconstructionist polytheist in the *filidecht* and *gentlidecht* traditions of Ireland (with further devotions to Romano-British, Gaulish, and Welsh deities), and a devotee of several divine ancestors and land spirits in the area of western Washington state. Lupus also occasionally participates in Shinto, Buddhist, and Hindu spiritual activities.

To date, Lupus' work has appeared in the Bibliotheca Alexandrina devotional anthologies for Artemis, Hekate, Isis and Serapis, Zeus, Pan, Thoth, Persephone, and the Near Eastern deities, with further forthcoming work to appear in the devotional volumes for the Dioskouroi, and Hephaistos, as well as others. Lupus is also in the process of co-editing a devotional anthology on cynocephalic deities for Bibliotheca Alexandrina, as well as an anthology on queer magic for Megalithica. Lupus' essays, fiction, and poetry have also appeared in *Datura: An Anthology of Esoteric Poeisis*, ed. Ruby Sara (Scarlet Imprint, 2010), *Spirit of Desire: Personal Explorations of Sacred Kink*, ed. Lee Harrington (Mystic Productions Press, 2010), and *Etched Offerings: Voices from the Cauldron of Story*, ed. Inanna Gabriel and C. Bryan Brown (Misanthrope Press, 2011). As you can imagine, many more pieces are in the works, and will appear in the future, if all goes well...

Lupus appears yearly at PantheaCon over President's Day weekend in San Jose, CA, and also runs public rituals in the greater Seattle area. Lupus also writes regularly on Antinous-related subjects at the Aedicula Antinoi blog (http://aediculaantinoi.wordpress.com/), and contributes a bi-weekly column to Patheos.com's Pagan Portal called "Queer I Stand."

The Syncretisms of Antinous

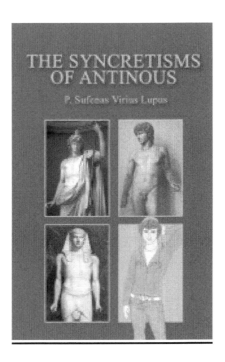

The Syncretisms of Antinous is an in-depth exploration of Antinous' relationship to other gods and heroes of the Greek, Roman, and Egyptian pantheons, both in antiquity and in later centuries. Antinous, the deified lover of the Roman Emperor Hadrian (117-138 CE), was syncretized to a large number of deities and heroes in his ancient cultus, and the process didn't stop when that cultus ended in the fifth century. Archaeologists, scholars, artists, and admirers of male beauty continued to link him to a great many figures from Greek, Roman, and Egyptian mythology. In this book, you will find out about the familiar as well as the more obscure syncretisms of Antinous, from Hermes to Herakles, Dionysos to the Dioskouroi, Apollon to Apis, Adonis to Attis, Pan to Poseidon, Achilleus to Aristaios, Endymion to Eunostos, Eros to Echmoun, and many more! You will also find resources to guide you in getting to know these syncretisms further, and ideas for devotional practices based upon them.

$20. ISBN 1456300458 http://www.createspace.com/3493936

Devotio Antinoo:
The Doctor's Notes, Volume One

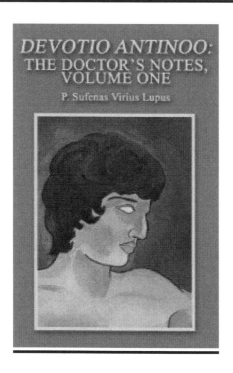

Devotio Antinoo: The Doctor's Notes, Volume One is a book that details all you'll need to start your own devotions to Antinous, including translated ancient texts and modern rituals of the Ekklesía Antínoou. The culmination of nearly ten years of research and devotion on the part of its author, *Devotio Antinoo* is presented now for the use of anyone who wishes to develop a devotional practice with Antinous, the gods with whom he was syncretized, Hadrian, other *Divi* and many more divine figures. Learn the holy days and festivals of the year, the hymns and prayers for both regular usage and specific occasions, the ancient texts that have survived in papyrus fragments, literary excerpts, inscriptions, and ideas on different devotional activities that can be performed as well. Everything you need to practice in the tradition of the Ekklesía Antínoou is contained in this book, and much more! With an exhaustive index, *Devotio Antinoo* will be an indispensible book in the library of any syncretistic polytheist!

$35. ISBN 1468004387   http://www.createspace.com/3735809

Coming soon from
THE RED LOTUS LIBRARY

Studium Antinoi: The Doctor's Notes, Volume Two Studies in theology and ethics, both new and from P. Sufenas Virius Lupus' old website, Aedicula Antinoi.

Something To Do: A Pagan Experiential Praxis Theology An argument for pagan theology in general from a radical perspective, and on the value of experiential, personal, and local polytheist religion.

Liber Dies Antinoi An in-depth detailing of the Ekklesía Antínoou calendar and the *Sancti*, formatted for use as a "book of days."

The Triads of Antinous A gnomic text for ease in understanding theological shorthand for Antinous and within Ekklesía Antínoou practice.

<u>COMING IN 2012 (and later)!</u>
For More Information, see
http://aediculaantinoi.wordpress.com/the-red-lotus-library/

Nysa Press was founded to publish the writings of H. Jeremiah Lewis and help promote the revival of Greco-Egyptian polytheism today. His books explore ancient history, literature, philosophy, mythology and the contemporary worship of the Greek and Egyptian deities.

From the Satyr's Mouth: Wit and Wisdom from an Opinionated Polytheist [ISBN: 1453643249]

In ancient Greece, satyrs were famed for their mocking criticism of societal conventions. H. Jeremiah Lewis brings that same spirit to a discussion of contemporary Pagan life and values in this latest collection of essays. Prepare to be challenged, informed, annoyed and hopefully entertained!

The Balance of the Greco-Egyptian [ISBN: 1442190337]

This collection of history and manifestations of polytheism. It system, information the afterlife, as well worship, ritual needed to begin today.

Two Lands: Writings on Polytheism

essays explores the long contemporary Greco-Egyptian provides overviews of the on theology, ethics, and as material on domestic forms, and the basics practicing the religion

Nysa Press was founded to publish the writings of H. Jeremiah Lewis and help promote the revival of Greco-Egyptian polytheism today. His books explore ancient history, literature, philosophy, mythology and the contemporary worship of the Greek and Egyptian deities.

Echoes of Alexandria: Poems and Stories
[ISBN: 1442190396]

This volume of poetry and short stories celebrates the author's undying love for the incomparable city of dreamers and the immortal gods and famous historical figures who once walked Alexandria's fabled streets. Included are hymns that have been used in actual worship, imaginative retellings of ancient stories, and modern myths set down for the first time.

Gods and Mortals: New Stories of Hellenic Polytheism [ISBN: 1449931294]

These are the stories of Hellenismos today. What it feels like to recognize the presence of the gods around you. To discover the mystery of the divine, the power of love, the joy of life, the pangs of grief, the loneliness that comes with belonging to a minority faith. You can read about ancient Greek religion in academic tomes - but none will tell you what it's like from the inside. For that, you must hear our stories, in our own words. Stories of gods and mortals.

Ecstatic [ISBN: 1463534655]

Who is Dionysos? There are as many answers to this enigmatic question as there are people asking it. For a significant portion of his life H. Jeremiah Lewis (perhaps better known by his religious name Sannion) has struggled to understand the ways and nature of this elusive ancient Greek deity of wine, vegetation, madness, drama, liberation and much else besides. In the course of his study and explorations he has produced an immense body of writing which has been gathered together in this unique volume for the first time ever. In addition to learning about Dionysian history, mythology, symbolism, and methods of worship both ancient and modern, the reader will gain a first-hand glimpse of what it's like to know and love a god as strange as Dionysos. Of special interest to Dionysians and occultists, this volume sees the first publication anywhere of a new oracular system involving the myths, symbols and associations of Dionysos with a concise explanation of how to use it.

For more information, see
http://www.thehouseofvines.com/nysapress.htm

To help promote the revival of traditional polytheistic traditions, Bibliotheca Alexandrina is publishing a series of volumes dedicated to the ancient Gods of Greece, Egypt and surrounding regions. Each volume contains essays, poetry, short fiction, rituals, artwork, et cetera focused on a particular divinity or group of divinities. These anthologies are a collaborative effort drawing on the combined resources of the modern Hellenic, Kemetic and broader polytheist communities, in the hope that we can come together to praise the Gods and share our diverse understandings, experiences and approaches to the divine. All of the proceeds from these books go to help promote the worship of the Gods, either by bringing out further volumes or through donation to charitable causes in Their names.

For more information, see
http://www.neosalexandria.org/publishing.htm

Current Titles from the Bibliotheca Alexandrina include:

 Written in Wine: A Devotional Anthology for Dionysos

The Phillupic Hymns by P. Sufenas Virius Lupus

 Unbound: A Devotional Anthology for Artemis

 Waters of Life: A Devotional Anthology for Isis and Serapis

 Bearing Torches: A Devotional Anthology for Hekate

 From Cave to Sky: A Devotional Anthology for Zeus

 Out of Arcadia: A Devotional Anthology in Honor of Pan

Anointed: A Devotional Anthology for the Deities of the Near and Middle East

 The Scribing Ibis: An Anthology of Pagan Fiction in Honor of Thoth

Queen of the Sacred Way: A Devotional Anthology in Honor of Persephone

And Coming Soon:

Devotional anthologies for Hephaistos, the Dioskouroi, Cynocephalic Deities, Hermes, Athena, Virgin Goddesses, Polytheist Science Fiction, and more!

159

Coming Soon from Misanthrope Press

Etched Offerings
Voices from the Cauldron of Story

An anthology of Pagan fiction

With an Introduction by:

Including stories by:

R. S. Bohn
P. Sufenas Virius Lupus
Cory Thomas Hutcheson

S. J. Tucker

and Llewellyn author
Kenny Klein

Misanthrope Press

Did You Like What You Read?

If you enjoyed this book, you might also like...

Sekhem Heka by Storm Constantine
ISBN: 978-1-905713-13-4 / MB0114
£12.99/$21.99 paperback
Drawing upon her experiences in Egyptian Magic and the energy healing systems of Reiki and Seichim, Storm Constantine has developed this new system to appeal to practitioners of both magic and energy healing.

Women's Voices in Magic edited by Brandy Williams
ISBN 978-1-905713-39-4 / MB0139
£11.99/$20.99 paperback
The essays in this book explode gender stereotypes and survey the spectrum of women's experiences in magic. Women are witches, but also ceremonial magicians, Satanists and sex magicians. Women dream, use intuition and make magical tools but they also argue, create ritual, and fiercely contest their right to achievement

Dancing With Spirits by Denny Sargent
ISBN 978-1-905713-52-3/MB0146
£10.99/$19.99 paperback
An intellectual but accessible 'travel guide through the history and fun reality of the most important Shinto and Buddhist festivals of Japan, featuring entertaining first-hand accounts of wild revels like Tanabata and Setsubun.

Ogam: Weaving Word Wisdom by Erynn Rowan Laurie
ISBN 978-1-905713-02-8/MB0110
£13.99/$22.99 paperback
An explanation of the history of ogam, with an introduction to each of the ogam and their origins and divination layouts. There's plenty more to the magic of ogam than divination, and *Ogam: Weaving Word Wisdom* makes it quite clear that if you thought you knew everything about ogam--you're in for a big surprise!

Talking About the Elephant edited by Lupa
978-1-905713-24-0/MB0125
£11.99 $20.99 paperback
Modern pagans draw from a variety of cultural wells. All too often the effects of this borrowing are ignored in lieu of "spiritual development". This book promotes constructive communication about issues surrounding cultural appropriation in neopaganism. The 19 essays cover a multitude of practices and topics.

Graeco-Egyptian Magic by Tony Mierzwicki
ISBN 978-1-905713-03-7/MB0103
£12.99 $21.99 paperback
Stemming from years of study this book outlines a daily practice involving planetary Hermeticism, drawn from the original texts and converted into a format that fits easily into the modern magician's practice.

Shades of Faith edited by Crystal Blanton
ISBN 978-1-905713-69-1 / MB0151
£10.99 $19.99 paperback
An anthology that addresses some of the challenges, stereotyping, frustrations, talents, history and beauties of being different within the racial constructs of typical Pagan or Wiccan groups.

Ecstatic Ritual by Brandy Williams
ISBN 978-1-905713-25-7 /MB0111
£10.99 $19.99 paperback
From ancient to modern times, people have looked to sexuality to aid them in connecting with the Divine.This book offers the reader clear, concise exercises and ritual forms which comprise a full understanding of sacred and magical sexuality.

Find these and the rest of our current lineup at http://www.immanion-press.com

Made in the USA
Lexington, KY
27 April 2013